Housekeeping Service in Hotels

Roy Hayter

Hospitality Training Foundation

MACMILLAN

First published 1997 by
MACMILLAN PRESS LTD
Houndmills, Basingstoke,
Hampshire RG21 6XS
and London
Companies and representatives
throughout the world

in association with

HOSPITALITY TRAINING
FOUNDATION
International House, High Street,
Ealing, London W5 5DB

ISBN 0–333–72537–9

Reprinted 1998

A catalogue record for this book is
available from the British Library

10 9 8 7 6 5 4 3 2
06 05 04 03 02 01 00 99 98

Graphics, design and typesetting
by the author

Printed in Great Britain by
Unwin Brothers Ltd, The Gresham
Press, Old Woking, Surrey
A member of the Martin's Printing
Group

Acknowledgements

Housekeeping Training Kits Steering Committee

Michael Bizley, Cleaning Industry Lead Body; Jacqui Davensac, St James Court Hotel; Mark Egan, Excelsior Hotel; Angela Jaquiss, Stratford upon Avon College; Alan Makinson, *Chairman of Committee*, Greenalls Group Hotels & Leisure; Ilsa Moore, London Marriott; Dave Saunders, Department for Education and Employment; Janis Smith, Southmeads NHS Trust; Ann Thunhurst, Chelmsford College

Reviewers

John Butler, Clavis Limited; Anne Davies, Lakefield Catering and Educational Centre, London; Sheila Perera, The Gleneagles Hotel and UK Housekeepers Association; Liz Smith-Mills, DiverseyLever and fellow members of the Yorkshire branch of the UK Housekeepers Association

Contributing industry procedures and other material

De Vere Hotels, Alan Makinson; De Vere Oulton Hall, Leeds, Claire Kenyon; DiverseyLever, Liz Smith-Mills; Friendly Hotels plc (for Comfort Inn and Quality Hotel), Brian Worthington; The Gleneagles Hotel, Sheila Perera; Going for Green; Jeyes UK; S C Johnson Professional; Principal Hotels, Gail Hunter; St David's Park Hotel & Golf Club, Nr Chester, Gail Powell; Simon Jersey Limited, Catherine Baroun; Sketchley; Swallow Royal Hotel, Bristol, Jane Sagar; The University of Sheffield, David McKown; Travel Inn, David Goodson; Vikan A/S (the trading name of KLEEN E QUIP (UK) LTD); Vileda LP; Whitbread Hotel Company, Mike Cowan

Industry piloting

The Angel Hotel, Cardiff, Petra Kops; Belton Woods Hotel, Varena Mason; Champneys Health Resort, Tring, Ingrid Watson; Crown Hotel, Scarborough, Geraldine Cook; De Vere Grand Harbour Hotel, Southampton, Paula Burston; Donnington Thistle Hotel, Julie Hales and Caroline Quentin; The Grand Hotel, Brighton, Peter Maskens and Julia Sinclair; Hythe Imperial, Julia Pickersgill; Lakefield Catering and Educational Centre, London, Anne Davies; Marcliffe at Pitfodels, Aberdeen, Eileen Booth; Petty France Hotel, Badminton, Shelley Spiller; St James Court Hotel, London, Sylvia Tsiampis; University of Kent Hospitality, Mavis Towl; University of Sheffield Residential Catering & Conference Services, Julia Cooke; Welcome Break Sarn Park Services, Chris Ellis Evans

Contents

Complaints

When a guest complains, put your own feelings to one side:

- be calm – even when what the guest says or does makes you angry, hurt, or embarrassed
- be professional – follow your hotel's complaints procedure.

When the complaint is dealt with well, the guest is likely to remain or become a regular customer. What is remembered is your efficiency and courtesy in dealing with the matter.

St. David's Park Hotel Golf Club

Complaint handling

Our goal is that there should be no cause for complaints, but obviously things go wrong sometimes. To turn negative situations into a positive outcome:

- when receiving a complaint, never show antagonism or anger: be professional and courteous at all times
- if the complaint is one you can deal with, e.g. 'You've brought me an extra hand towel when I asked for a bath sheet', then do so, apologising for the inconvenience
- if the complaint is more serious, e.g. 'I've been waiting over two hours for my laundry to be returned, and these aren't my shirts, I refuse to pay this bill', apologise and inform the guest that your head of department or the duty manager (give the name of the person) will investigate and report to the guest.

The guests who don't complain

Many guests don't complain formally. But they don't come back again. And usually they tell other people of what went wrong or the poor service, so the hotel loses these customers as well.

You can help keep these guests by being aware when something is not right, and then acting as you do for a formal complaint. Signals of displeasure include:

- what is said – 'We had a lot of trouble getting to sleep' (enquiries might reveal that noisy central heating was to blame – you can apologise, report it to maintenance, and if the problem can't be fixed, the guests can be moved)
- what is not said – 'Well, OK' in answer to your question 'I hope your room is comfortable?' (the guests expected a sea-view, but the option was not explained at the time they booked – reception could offer to move the guests to a better room)
- unhappy, irritated, or angry tone in the voice, expression on the face, or movement of the body.

How to deal with complaints

1. Listen to the complaint fully. Do not interrupt, even when you will be asking someone else to handle the situation.

2. Apologise properly and sincerely, but do not admit that any person or the hotel is at fault.

3. Do not make excuses or blame anyone else.

4. Never argue or disagree. React as if the guest is right, even when you believe otherwise.

5. Keep calm and remain polite.

6. Never offer something you cannot provide – consider, for example, what would happen if you agree to move the guest to another room, and reception had already allocated that room.

7. Thank the guest for bringing the matter to your attention – said with feeling, this shows that you are genuine in your efforts to put things right.

Telephone courtesy

When you use the telephone at work, the impression you give – of yourself, of the housekeeping department, of the hotel – depends on what you say and how you say it. The person at the other end of the phone line – who may be a guest, a supplier, a boss or someone else from work – can't see your smart uniform or friendly smile.

Customer care

Use customers' names, and give a pleasant greeting
... it makes them feel important.

Ask questions
... it encourages them to give you more information.

Ask how you can help
... it shows you are interested.

Apologise if you have to keep people waiting
... it is appreciated.

Offer someone else's help if the person they want is not available
... it can save everyone's time and shows concern.

Empathise with people
... e.g. 'I understand why you feel...'

Avoid jargon
... it causes misunderstanding and embarrassment.

Thank them for their custom
... they could easily have chosen another hotel.

How to answer the phone

1 Answer the telephone quickly. If it has been ringing for a while, perhaps because you were elsewhere, apologise for keeping the caller waiting.

2 Greet the caller in a friendly way. If you say 'Good morning', sound as if you mean it.

3 Identify yourself and offer to help. If your hotel has one, use the standard greeting, e.g. 'This is Sarah of housekeeping speaking, the Manor House, how may I help you?' (for an internal call, you would not need to say your hotel name).

4 At the end of the call, thank the person and say goodbye.

Good morning, housekeeping. Sheila speaking. How may I help you?

The Gleneagles Hotel
Guest skills

When you pass or approach a guest, look at the guest, smile and say 'Good morning, Sir', 'Good afternoon, Madam', 'Hello young lady', etc. as appropriate for the time of day and age of the guest. Use the guest's name if you know it: on your section sheet, names are listed against the number of each guest room.

Remember, guests are here to enjoy themselves, and are paying for it. By looking pleasant, you help create a happy, relaxed atmosphere for guests. And you help make the work of everyone in the hotel more rewarding and enjoyable.

Taking messages

Date and time message taken	*Monday 18 April. 10.30 am*
Who it is for	*TO: Mrs Khan*
Who it is from: give company name if business call	*Nigel Crowe, from Nelson Cleaners phoned.* — Write clearly
Reason for calling or message	*He wants to come and look at the carpets which have to be cleaned, to give you an estimate.*
Phone number to return call. Or other means of contact, e.g. fax number	*Please call him on: 01234 5678910 between 9 am and 1 pm on Tuesday or Wednesday.* — Details of caller's availability, if appropriate
Your name	*Betty*

Other hints on using the phone

Speak directly into the telephone mouthpiece. Use your normal tone of voice and accent. If the caller has trouble hearing, speak a little more slowly and loudly (but don't shout).

Be clear

Use simple, everyday language. Avoid slang or swear words which the other person may find offensive. Do not use industry or housekeeping terms (e.g. 'no shows', 'chance lets') which are meaningless to most guests. (For your own use, there is an explanation of these terms on page 36.)

Listen

Listen carefully, and don't interrupt. Give your full attention to the conversation. Ask questions when you need to find out more.

Check facts

Check that you have understood facts correctly, e.g. room and telephone numbers, names of guests (and how to pronounce them), the caller's name and company.

Courtesy counts

If you have to ask the caller to hold on while you get someone, or find out information:

- apologise
- say how long you will be
- keep the caller informed if there is a delay
- if the wait is more than a few minutes, offer to call back.

Personal touch

Use the caller's name from time to time. This gives a personal touch.

Transferring the call

Explain to the caller what you are doing.

When your colleague answers, say who is on the line and, briefly, what the call is about.

If the phone is not answered quickly, get back to the caller, apologise, offer to keep trying or to take a message. You may be able to put the caller through to someone else who can help, or try another extension. If so, explain what you are doing.

They were bringing the housekeeper to the phone

Making a call

Think about what you are going to say, and have ready any information you need.

Ask for the person or department you want to speak to, and say who you are and where you are from. Be ready to repeat this if you get transferred to someone else.

Meeting guests

- Always acknowledge guests you meet, make eye contact and smile.
- Greet with the courtesy of the day, 'Good morning/ afternoon'.
- Be courteous, hold doors open.
- Be aware of the additional facilities/services the hotel offers and local amenities.
- If you don't know the answer, direct the guest to reception.

Guests with special needs

- Only vary standard procedure if the guest requests it.
- Speak at normal volume and speed, do not exaggerate lip movements.
- Offer a pen and pad, plus something to lean on (e.g. clipboard) to write down information when communication is difficult.
- Offer additional help, e.g. with luggage, mobility, reading, writing, lighting.
- Do whatever is requested without drawing attention to the guest.
- Be aware of additional facilities/services your hotel offers disabled guests, e.g. disabled bedrooms, Braille/ large print information, portable ramps.
- Be aware of room numbers of disabled guests, so you can provide help in the event of an evacuation.

Work as a team

Try to **TEAM**

T	hank
E	xplain
A	pologise
M	ention

be **WORK**

W	elcoming
O	pen
R	espectful
K	een

Your work is more enjoyable, and the job goes better, when you get on well with the people there. When you do your job well, so can those who work with you. And the guests get the best service.

Building a strong team

Everyone contributes to good teamwork. Everyone benefits from a strong team. Here are some of the things you can do.

Be pleasant to work with

Be polite and good-tempered to everyone, even when you're under pressure. It takes little effort to say 'please' and 'thank you'. If you have to interrupt what someone is doing, or have kept the person waiting, say 'sorry'.

Be ready to help

Some of the tasks you find easy may be difficult to others, especially to someone new to the job. A few words of explanation, or a helping hand can make all the difference and not delay your work at all.

Do your job properly

Do your job to the best of your ability. Don't leave tasks unfinished or badly done. No one appreciates having to do your job as well as their own.

Be punctual

Get to work on time. If you are delayed or ill, telephone your supervisor as soon as possible. Knowing what's happened makes it easier to rearrange duties. It also stops people worrying unnecessarily.

Be understanding

Consider, and respect, other points of view, even if you don't agree with them. There may be a policy or business reason why some things are done differently from your previous experience.

What you wear

Your work clothes should give the right impression to guests, and be comfortable, practical and safe. Avoid accessories and jewellery which might get caught on things. After changing into uniform, leave your outdoor clothing and footwear in the place provided (e.g. locker in the staff changing room).

Looking after your feet

You spend long hours on your feet. Wear comfortable shoes that will not slip, which cover your whole foot and which protect your toes against dropped objects. Wash your feet every day, and keep your toe nails trimmed. Change socks or stockings daily.

How you look

Long flowing hair is not suitable at work. It might get trapped in furniture you are cleaning. Lengths of hair are likely to fall on to surfaces. There is usually a rule that long hair must be tied back, and you may be asked to wear a cap.

Daily washing will keep your hair clean and in healthy condition.

Personal hygiene

Keep yourself clean and fresh. The body secretes moisture constantly through sweat glands located all over it. You will perspire more working under pressure in warm rooms. Sweat has no odour and evaporates quickly. But the bacteria which live on the perspiration do smell – especially under your arms, where sweat cannot evaporate freely. A daily bath or shower and a good deodorant or antiperspirant are the best protection.

Your hands

Pay special attention to your hands. Your fingernails should be clean and neatly trimmed. Nail varnish is best avoided. Apply a hand cream regularly to help keep your hands soft and presentable.

Always wash your hands:

- before going on duty
- after a break
- after using the toilet
- after touching anything which is soiled.

Use plenty of hot water and soap, rinse your hands, then dry them well.

Keep those germs to yourself

If you are about to sneeze, cough, or blow your nose:

- cover your nose and mouth with a paper tissue
- face away from other people, clean surfaces, your trolley, etc.
- wash your hands afterwards.

Control any impulse to lick your fingers, bite your nails, touch your nose, mouth or hair, or spit.

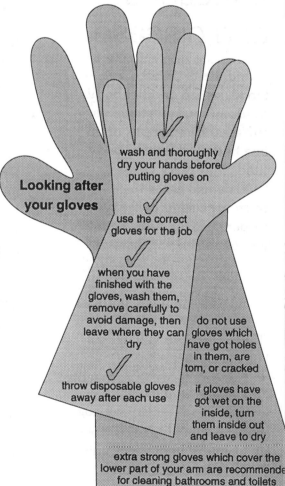

Looking after your gloves

wash and thoroughly dry your hands before putting gloves on

use the correct gloves for the job

when you have finished with the gloves, wash them, remove carefully to avoid damage, then leave where they can dry

do not use gloves which have got holes in them, are torn, or cracked

throw disposable gloves away after each use

if gloves have got wet on the inside, turn them inside out and leave to dry

extra strong gloves which cover the lower part of your arm are recommended for cleaning bathrooms and toilets

Work safely

Everyone at work, however junior their position, full-time, part-time or casual, has a duty to protect the health and safety of those around them. This is a moral responsibility and a matter of law.

Safety first

Inattention, forgetting, lack of care and bad habits cause workplace accidents. One of these may not be serious. But an unlucky chain of events and one or more errors can combine with fatal results.

When there are many pressures on you and others in a busy workplace, it is not easy to maintain the highest safety standards. Nevertheless – and whatever the effort involved – safety has to be a top priority.

Learn safety

You will be trained or instructed on the safe way of using equipment and cleaners. Don't be afraid to ask questions.

Never put yourself and others in danger and risk damaging the equipment, by:

- attempting to use something you are not familiar with
- saying you have had training when you haven't
- acting the expert when colleagues can't get equipment to work.

What can happen

Your employer can dismiss you without notice for serious breaches of health and safety procedures. You might find yourself in court. For your employer, the consequences could include a big fine, huge legal bill and bad publicity.

SWALLOW ROYAL HOTEL
B R I S T O L

Always think safety

Awareness is an essential part of every employee's contribution to the safety of staff and guests alike.

Follow the guidelines and training you have been given. Never take short cuts.

Broken glass

- With a dustpan and brush, collect large pieces of glass and place in your red metal bin.
- Vacuum small fragments.
- Wash floor where breakage occurred. Let it dry. Wash once again.
- Ensure that you tell a floor housekeeper.

Sanitary waste

- Place used sanibags in the yellow bag on your trolley. At the end of duty, place the bag in the chemical waste bin.
- Never put sanibags among other waste.
- Never put sanibags in your pantry or leave them on your trolley.

Use cleaning agents safely

Some of the cleaners you use are hazardous. Sometimes the harm is not immediate, but regular contact can lead to problems. If you do not wear gloves when using a general purpose cleaner, for example, your skin will become very dry and you may get dermatitis.

From the label and workplace instructions and training, you will get help on how to use cleaners safely. Pay careful attention to this guidance at all times.

Rules of safety

1 Wear protective clothing as instructed:

   - gloves of the right type, e.g. long gloves for bathroom cleaning so that your arms are also protected

   - face mask if there is a risk of splashing

   - goggles if there is a risk of eye contact

   - uniform including apron, as specified in your workplace.

2 Only use cleaners for the purpose specified, and in the recommended quantity and strength:

   - never mix different cleaners

   - do not use a succession of different cleaners on the same surface, without rinsing well in between

   - when diluting cleaners, use the measures provided (e.g. cap, scoop or measuring cup) – never guess quantities

   - mix with cold/warm/ hot water as stated

   - to dilute, add the concentrated cleaner to the water – this reduces the risk of splashing neat cleaner on yourself or nearby surfaces, and produces less foam.

3 Store cleaners in their original container, or a container reserved for that type of cleaning agent. All containers must be clearly labelled with the product and its instructions for use.

4 Never put cleaners in any container which might be, or is sometimes used to hold food or drink such as an empty drinks bottle, a cup, or glass. Guests, residents and staff of hotels, hospitals and homes for the elderly have suffered serious injury, and in some cases lost their lives, because this safety rule has been broken.

5 Know what to do if you should accidentally come into contact with a cleaner which is an irritant or corrosive. Take note of the warning label and safety instructions on the container:

   - in case of contact with eyes or skin – e.g. rinse immediately with plenty of water and seek medical advice

   - if swallowed – e.g. drink plenty of milk or water and seek medical advice immediately

   - if spilled on your clothing – e.g. take off any contaminated clothing immediately.

what

What does it mean?

COSHH The Control of Substances Hazardous to Health (COSHH) Regulations 1994. Sets out the measures that your employer and you as an employee have to take when storing and using cleaning materials and other substances that may be harmful.

Corrosive Warning label on substances which can destroy solid substances. On contact with your skin or any other part of your body, they are likely to cause severe burns.

Harmful or **irritant** Warning label on substances which are a limited health risk. Contact with such substances may cause inflammation and irritation – perhaps with repeated or prolonged contact.

Toxic or **Very toxic** Warning label on substances which may cause serious health risk or even death if breathed in, swallowed or in contact with your skin or eyes.

Only use for purpose specified

Follow instructions for use carefully

Check for special instructions

Follow timings

Store safely

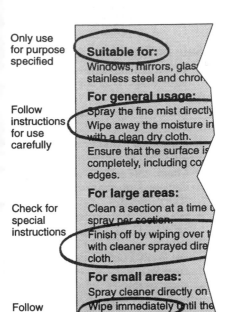

Suitable for:
Windows, mirrors, glass, stainless steel and chro...

For general usage:
Spray the fine mist directly...
Wipe away the moisture in... with a clean dry cloth.
Ensure that the surface is... completely, including co... edges.

For large areas:
Clean a section at a time... spray per section.
Finish off by wiping over... with cleaner sprayed dire... cloth.

For small areas:
Spray cleaner directly on...
Wipe immediately until the... clean and clear.

Storage:
Glass cleaner can be saf... stored with its trigger spr...
Simply turn the nozzle t... 'off' position and store unti... again.

Instructions with thanks to S C Johnson Professional

What to look for and report

Before using electrical cleaning equipment, check for these visual signs

When servicing guest rooms, check hairdryers, kettles, TVs, trouser presses, etc. for these visual signs

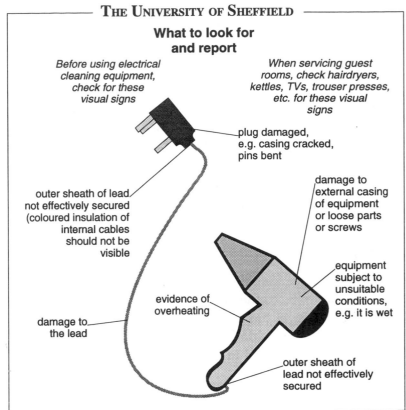

plug damaged, e.g. casing cracked, pins bent

damage to external casing of equipment or loose parts or screws

outer sheath of lead not effectively secured (coloured insulation of internal cables should not be visible)

equipment subject to unsuitable conditions, e.g. it is wet

evidence of overheating

damage to the lead

outer sheath of lead not effectively secured

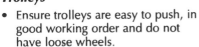

DE VERE HOTELS

Housekeeping safety

We all have a responsibility for the safety of everyone in our hotels – guests, contractors *and* fellow employees. Help us to make your hotel a safe place to be in.

Using buckets

- Do not overfill – particularly with hot water.
- Keep away from electrical equipment and entrances and exits.
- Do not leave on stairways.

Using vacuum cleaners, floor scrubbers and polishers

- Avoid trailing leads across entrances and exits.
- Empty vacuum cleaners regularly.
- Store equipment safely and securely.
- Do not operate electrical equipment with wet hands.
- Do not balance such equipment on stairways.

Trolleys

- Ensure trolleys are easy to push, in good working order and do not have loose wheels.
- Do not overload trolleys, especially with chemicals.
- Do not empty broken glass or crockery in the plastic waste bag.
- Take care when disposing of smoking waste – do not empty ashtrays into plastic bags or cardboard boxes.

Linen skips

- Position skips in a safe place in corridors, not obstructing fire exits or fire doors.
- Empty skips at regular intervals.
- Never put rubbish in skips: skips are for dirty linen only.
- Remove skips from corridors when not in use.

Using cleaning agents

- Do not leave cleaning solutions unattended – particularly where children could be present.
- Cleaners should not be mixed, either on the article to be cleaned or in a separate container.
- Always use the correct material on the correct surface. Incorrect use damages surfaces.
- When using aerosols or sprays, check that you are not pointing the spray into your face (or anyone else's). There is a directional arrow on top of the nozzle to avoid confusion.
- Always replace tops and caps properly after use.
- Wipe up any spilled cleaning material immediately.

YOU NEVER PLAN TO HAVE AN ACCIDENT BUT YOU CAN PLAN TO PREVENT ONE!

Use fire fighting equipment

In every corridor, public room and service area, you will find at least one fire extinguisher. This is for fighting small fires. Get to know the positions of extinguishers, how they should be used and what fires they are suitable for:

- *public areas* – water extinguishers or a fire hose or automatic fire sprinklers

- *service areas* where there is electrical equipment – carbon dioxide or powder extinguishers, sometimes foam extinguishers (if of suitable type)

- *floor service kitchens* – fire blanket, foam or powder extinguisher.

Remember, using the wrong extinguisher can make the fire worse.

Never put yourself at risk by attempting to fight a fire. This may be difficult to judge, but do not be tempted to play the hero. The rule is:

IF IN DOUBT, DON'T.

Concentrate on raising the alarm and helping guests – and anyone else unfamiliar with the layout of the building or in difficulty – leave the building safely.

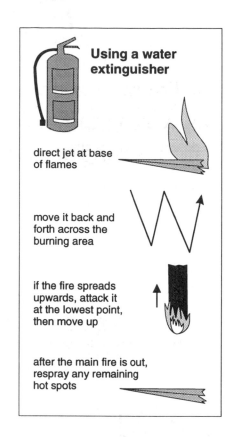

Using a water extinguisher

direct jet at base of flames

move it back and forth across the burning area

if the fire spreads upwards, attack it at the lowest point, then move up

after the main fire is out, respray any remaining hot spots

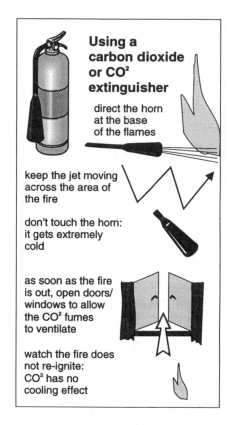

Using a carbon dioxide or CO_2 extinguisher

direct the horn at the base of the flames

keep the jet moving across the area of the fire

don't touch the horn: it gets extremely cold

as soon as the fire is out, open doors/ windows to allow the CO_2 fumes to ventilate

watch the fire does not re-ignite: CO_2 has no cooling effect

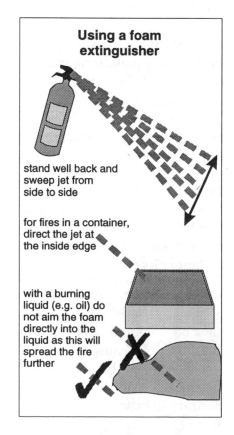

Using a foam extinguisher

stand well back and sweep jet from side to side

for fires in a container, direct the jet at the inside edge

with a burning liquid (e.g. oil) do not aim the foam directly into the liquid as this will spread the fire further

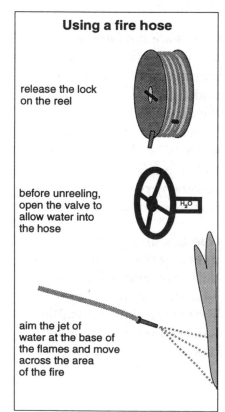

Using a fire hose

release the lock on the reel

before unreeling, open the valve to allow water into the hose

aim the jet of water at the base of the flames and move across the area of the fire

What extinguisher to use

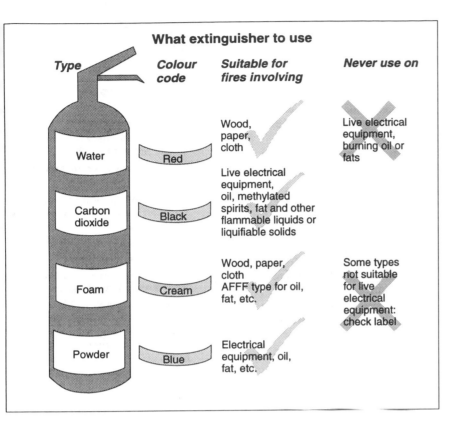

Type	Colour code	Suitable for fires involving	Never use on
Water	Red	Wood, paper, cloth ✓	Live electrical equipment, burning oil or fats ✗
Carbon dioxide	Black	Live electrical equipment, oil, methylated spirits, fat and other flammable liquids or liquifiable solids	
Foam	Cream	Wood, paper, cloth AFFF type for oil, fat, etc. ✓	Some types not suitable for live electrical equipment: check label ✗
Powder	Blue	Electrical equipment, oil, fat, etc. ✓	

Change to colour-coding

New extinguishers since 1997 are one colour only, red, to make them standard throughout the EC. The extinguisher may have a band or label of a different colour, i.e. black, cream or blue, to indicate the contents.

The body of extinguishers bought before these regulations came into force, will be all red, black, cream or blue, depending on the type. Such extinguishers need only be changed at the end of their useful life, or if they are used in the same location as new extinguishers.

Using a powder extinguisher

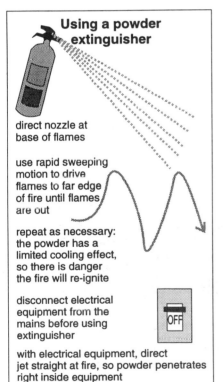

direct nozzle at base of flames

use rapid sweeping motion to drive flames to far edge of fire until flames are out

repeat as necessary: the powder has a limited cooling effect, so there is danger the fire will re-ignite

disconnect electrical equipment from the mains before using extinguisher

with electrical equipment, direct jet straight at fire, so powder penetrates right inside equipment

Fire signs and notices

These are there to protect you and everyone else in the building. Many fires cause great damage because people ignore the notice saying FIRE DOOR KEEP SHUT. Many people have been injured or lost their lives in fires because emergency exits have not been kept clear, or the doors locked, contrary to instructions.

FIRE INSTRUCTIONS FOR GUESTS

IF YOU DISCOVER A FIRE

Sound the alarm by operating the nearest fire alarm operating point, which is ON THE LANDING

ON HEARING THE FIRE ALARM

(The alarm in these premises is BELLS)

By night

1. Put on a dressing gown and shoes
2. DO NOT STOP to dress fully or to collect personal belongings
3. Ensure that all occupants of your room are awake
4. Leave the building by the nearest available escape route and go to the assembly point which is the CAR SHOW-ROOM OPPOSITE THE HOTEL shutting all doors behind you

By day

Go at once to the assembly point shutting all doors behind you

DO NOT RE-ENTER THE BUILDING

back if you pick up a light object expecting it to be heavy.

5 Look at the object and see how it can be held:

– a bulky item may be difficult to hold and control, and make it harder to see where you are going

– smooth sides, round surfaces, greasy hands and wearing gloves all make your grip less secure.

6 Check for hazards that will make the task more difficult, e.g.:

– narrow, steep stairs

– low ceilings

– uneven floors.

Make the task lighter

7 Use a trolley and the service lift where possible.

8 Divide large loads into smaller or less bulky batches. If this means making many journeys you may need to have a break.

Get help

9 If you don't feel it safe to proceed, get the assistance of a colleague.

10 To avoid confusion when working with another person, agree in advance who should give the instructions, and who will take the load.

How to lift and carry

get close to the load, feet slightly apart to give a stable base

hands as nearly level with the waist as possible

keep your back straight – tucking in your chin helps

don't bend your knees fully, as this will leave little power to lift

keep shoulders level and facing in the same direction as the hips

keep a firm grip

move smoothly, keeping control of the load

use your feet if you need to turn, don't twist your body

place the load down, then if necessary adjust its position

check the load won't fall over, roll, etc.

What you can safely handle

your physical strength – this is less if you have done a lot of carrying already, are tired or unwell or pregnant, for example

weight of object – test the weight by lifting one corner, or lifting the object a short distance then putting it down again

the shape of the object – a bulky item is often difficult to hold and control, and it might be less easy to see where you are going

how the object can be held – smooth sides, round surfaces, greasy hands, wearing gloves, these make your grip less secure

how far the object has to be moved – to get it into a carrying position (from a shelf at waist height is easier than from the floor), and to take it to its destination

in what conditions you are working – wet floors, steep stairs, low ceilings, etc. make the task harder

Your trolley

KEPT
clean
tidy
running smoothly
safely loaded
STOCKED
with what you require
to reduce the need
for fetching and carrying

Security matters

As you go about your work duties, take notice of what is going on around you. Report anything suspicious to a house-keeper, security officer or the manager.

You're the expert

In the areas of the building you work in regularly, you know much better than anyone else what should or shouldn't be there. Don't leave it to someone else to report the problem.

Why security matters

Hotels are popular targets for the dishonest and other troublemakers. By acting as if they are a genuine guest, they hope to go unnoticed. They are quick to take advantage of guests and staff who:

- are too trusting or careless
- or don't want to get involved.

ACTING AS A GENUINE GUEST, THEY HOPE TO GO UNNOTICED!!

Another security problem is controlling what guests get up to. This may be relatively harmless, like stealing an ashtray from their room.

Much more serious is when guests:

- steal valuable hotel property or the property of other guests
- take prostitutes into their hotel room
- get violent or abusive, or otherwise threaten the personal safety of guests or staff.

Tell your supervisor about:

✓ door locked from the inside, and no answer when you knock

✓ stayover guests who leave a DO NOT DISTURB notice on the door all day

✓ a DO NOT DISTURB notice still in place after the time when rooms must be vacated

PLEASE DO NOT DISTURB

✓ guests who tell you they don't want their room serviced

Don't bother, we'll clean the room

✓ if you find a door open which should be locked, or see other signs that suggest someone has gained access without authority

Suspicious people

If you see someone in a place they shouldn't be or acting suspiciously, ask politely:

- 'Can I help?'
- or 'May I see your key card, then I can help you find your room?'

This gives the person who has made a genuine mistake, the chance to explain. A dishonest person knows that you are suspicious and will report him or her.

Avoid direct questions such as 'What are you doing here?' or 'Are you lost?'. These may offend the genuine guest. And they are unlikely to get a useful reply from someone up to no good.

Suspicious items

If you see a suspicious item:

- do not touch it yourself or let anyone else do so
- call for help from management or security officers
- tell them calmly and accurately where the item is located, and why you think it is suspicious. They will get in touch with the emergency services.

Missing items

When you service guest rooms and public areas, be on the look out for anything missing. Are the correct number of towels still in the room? Is the remote control for the TV (and the TV itself) there?

If you think something has been removed, let your supervisor know straight away, as the guests may not have checked out. Besides, there may be a reason why the item has gone – perhaps the correct number of towels were not put in the room by error, or the 'stolen' TV has in fact gone for repair.

Don't make accusations

Avoid saying anything which might be taken as an accusation, if you meet guests who appear to have removed hotel property. Instead, find a way of alerting your supervisor without the guests becoming suspicious.

For example, you might say: 'Oh, I'm glad to see you, the manager wants to follow up the enquiry you made about our leisure club. Would you mind having a seat for a few moments, while I call her (or him)?' Remain with the guests until the manager arrives, chatting pleasantly about the weather or any similar, uncontroversial topic.

Dealing with a death

If you are the first to discover a guest has died (or appears to be dead):

- do not touch the body or anything in the room
- remain calm
- leave the room at once, hang the DO NOT DISTURB sign and lock the door
- report the matter immediately to someone in authority, e.g. the executive housekeeper, general manager, security officer (or do this via the hotel telephone operator)
- do not say anything to other guests or colleagues which might upset or alarm them
- do not speak about the incident outside work (except to a professional counsellor, if necessary). Gossip or press reports about a death in your hotel may harm the business.

The experience may leave you suffering from shock, perhaps not immediately, but some time afterwards. Seek the help of your supervisor or manager initially, and from a professional counsellor if you remain disturbed.

Security rules

Always follow security rules. These may include:

- which entrances and areas of the building you can use
- times for collecting linen and housekeeping supplies
- procedure for accepting deliveries
- arrangements for dealing with tradespeople and other visitors.

Never let anyone persuade you to 'bend the rules'. If you use your key to let someone into a bedroom, what will you say when the real guest turns up later to find valuable possessions gone?

Fire exits should never be locked or closed off in such a way that they cannot be used in an emergency.

DE VERE
OULTON HALL
★★★★
LEEDS

Key security
- You must sign for your keys at the beginning of each shift and sign them back in at the end.
- Keep keys on your person throughout the day.
- Never let anyone into a room unless they produce satisfactory proof of identity, i.e. the key card for that room.
- If you find any keys, hand them to the floor or head housekeeper immediately.
- Never leave open more than one door at a time, and only while you are in the room.

Key security

You will be asked to sign keys in and out. If you lend your keys to another room attendant and they go missing, it will be your responsibility, since the keys were signed out to you.

Looking after keys

Always keep keys on your person: hanging from your belt, or in a pocket. Do not leave keys in the guest room door while you clean a room, or on your trolley.

Report missing keys as soon as you discover their loss.

Missing keys are a great worry

Have the keys been taken by someone planning a break-in? If the keys turn up later, has someone had copies made? If the keys are found by chance, might they be used dishonestly? Changing the locks (which may be the only solution) is expensive.

Storage areas

When you have access to a storeroom or other area which is kept locked, you are responsible for leaving it locked. Even if you have to leave the room temporarily, relock it.

Found guest room keys

If you find a guest room key left in the door or somewhere in the room:

- put the key in the lock box on your trolley, your pocket or some other safe place
- phone reception to say you have the keys (which otherwise might be thought lost)
- return the keys before you go off duty or sooner if reception ask.

KEEP KEYS SAFE · Keep on you · Do not lend · Report missing keys · Report found keys

---

what
What does it mean?

Double locked room Cannot be opened with a floor master key (some types of lock can be locked so that only the grand master key will open them.)

Floor master key Opens all rooms on a particular floor or section of the hotel.

Grand master key Opens all rooms in the hotel and any doors which have been double locked.

PRINCIPAL
H O T E L S

Security

In stayover rooms, only open drawers or wardrobes if you need to replenish supplies (e.g. of laundry bags).

When dealing with room moves, only move the guest's personal belongings if a housekeeper is present while you are doing this.

Only open one bedroom at a time when servicing rooms. Never prop open a row of doors, particularly of stayovers.

Lost property

All lost property, no matter how minor, must be handed in.

Hand in valuable lost property immediately to the housekeeper, who will lock it in the safe.

Minor lost property can be safely kept, to hand in at the end of your shift.

Always record: date lost property found, room number, description of item, who found.

Your own security

It is safer – and easier – to clean rooms when the guests are elsewhere. Your house-keeper will tell you what to do in other situations. For example:

- if the guest returns while you are cleaning the room, it may be best to arrange a time when you can return to finish your tasks

- or, there may be a rule that two people must clean rooms when guests are in the room at the same time.

Don't put yourself at risk. Guests may make improper suggestions, or report that you have done so (even though you have done no such thing).

Protect guest property

Never use your key to let guests into a room. One possible exception is where you know the guest well and which room he or she is in. This may happen with long-term guests, VIPs, or perhaps in a small hotel.

Not using your key to open a guest's room

If a guest asks you to open the room with your key:

- apologise and say that you are not allowed to do this

- explain politely that the guest must ask at reception for another key or key card

- offer to phone reception with the guest's name, so he or she can be dealt with quickly.

Guests may get angry when you refuse to unlock the room, or try some other tactic to persuade you. Be firm. Explain that it is a strict rule, to protect the security of guests.

Checking before letting guests enter a room you are cleaning

If guests come into a room you are cleaning, saying that it is their room, ask to see the key or key card.

Found Room 326
10 May. 9.30 am

If they are unable to produce the correct key or key card for the room, ask them to go to reception. Alert reception as soon as the guest is out of earshot. The person may not be a genuine guest.

Lost property

When you find clothing, shoes or any of the other things that guests leave behind in their room, remove the item(s) to a safe place, e.g. the housekeeper's office. Do this as soon as possible as the owner may still be in the building. Money, travel tickets, jewellery, keys and other valuable items must be handed in to your supervisor or manager immediately.

Complete the lost property form or leave a note with the lost property of when you found it and where. This information helps identify the owner.

If guests come to you about lost property, direct them to where they can get help, e.g. reception. If the housekeeper or manager has to be found, show the guests to a place where they can wait in comfort. You may know the guests and be able to tell them that their child's teddy bear is safe. With valuable items, it is better not to indicate what you know. Leave others to establish that the claim is genuine.

Why and how you clean

Something which is not clean looks unpleasant. It gives guests a poor impression. A build-up of dirt is a hygiene risk – bacteria and pests thrive in these conditions. It may damage surfaces, e.g. leaving a permanent stain. It may be a safety risk.

Why clean?

Surfaces are cleaned not just because they look dirty. Certainly it is important to remove all visible dirt, but cleaning also helps remove bacteria that cannot be seen. This is especially so in bathrooms.

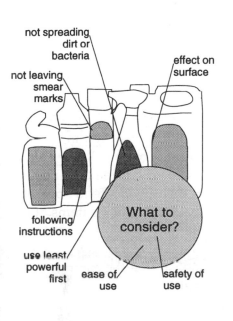

not spreading dirt or bacteria

not leaving smear marks

effect on surface

following instructions

What to consider?

use least powerful first

ease of use

safety of use

What you use?

The aim is to remove dirt as easily, quickly and thoroughly as possible. There should be no harm done to the item you are cleaning. Nor any harm to yourself, through contact with cleaning substances that damage your skin or eyes, or by breathing in harmful fumes.

There should be no risk of moving the dirt elsewhere. Cleaning methods must not send fine dust up into the air, to settle on surfaces you have already dusted. Nor should they transfer bacteria from one place (e.g. a cloth used to clean the toilet seat) to another (e.g. the bathroom door handle, were the same cloth to be wrongly used).

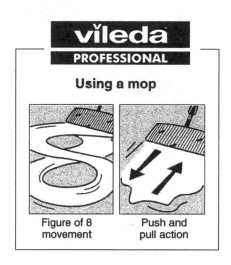

vĭleda
PROFESSIONAL

Using a mop

Figure of 8 movement

Push and pull action

How you clean

The cleaning materials and equipment you are provided with, and the instructions for their use, are designed to remove dirt effectively.

The diagrams overleaf introduce the main methods of cleaning. More information is given in later sections of the book.

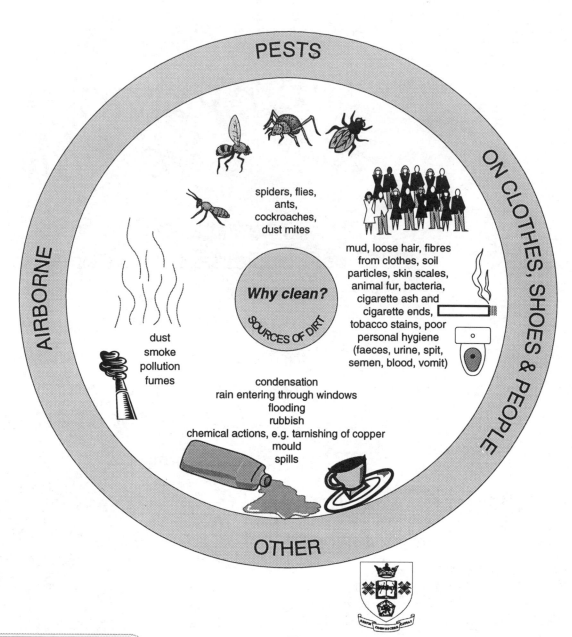

PESTS

ON CLOTHES, SHOES & PEOPLE

AIRBORNE

OTHER

spiders, flies, ants, cockroaches, dust mites

mud, loose hair, fibres from clothes, soil particles, skin scales, animal fur, bacteria, cigarette ash and cigarette ends, tobacco stains, poor personal hygiene (faeces, urine, spit, semen, blood, vomit)

Why clean?
SOURCES OF DIRT

dust
smoke
pollution
fumes

condensation
rain entering through windows
flooding
rubbish
chemical actions, e.g. tarnishing of copper
mould
spills

THE UNIVERSITY OF SHEFFIELD

what
What does it mean?

Aids Acquired Immune Deficiency Syndrome. The body loses its ability to fight infection.

Contaminated Carrying micro-organisms likely to cause illness.

Cross contamination Transfer of bacteria from one surface or item to another.

HIV Human Immunodeficiency Virus. HIV is carried in the blood and other body fluids of an infected person. It breaks down the body's resistance to infection.

Microorganism Any small living organism, including bacteria and viruses. **Pathogenic** micro-organisms cause disease.

Dusting
- use a dry, lint free duster
- dust from top to bottom, using smooth strokes
- clean duster as needed so as not to move dust from place to place
- do not flick duster

Damp dusting
- use a cloth dampened with cleaner, then wrung almost dry
- wipe surface from top to bottom, using smooth strokes
- wash duster as needed

Washing
- apply cleaner using a cloth, then remove dirt by wiping with cloth, turning the cloth frequently
- rinse cloth in cleaning solution to remove dirt as often as necessary
- apply clean rinse water
- wipe dry with a clean cloth

Polishing
- surface should be previously damp dusted and allowed to dry
- apply sparingly, avoid applying polish to adjacent surfaces
- if using an aerosol polish containing silicone, spray polish on to cloth, then apply
- when dry, buff to a high sheen

Safety
- avoid splashes of cleaner on furniture, curtains or floors
- wipe any splashes from floor immediately
- do not spray an aerosol on to furniture standing on a hard floor, as polish may go on the floor making it slippery

Care of equipment
- wash dusters and cloths
- wash buckets, wipe dry and store upside down

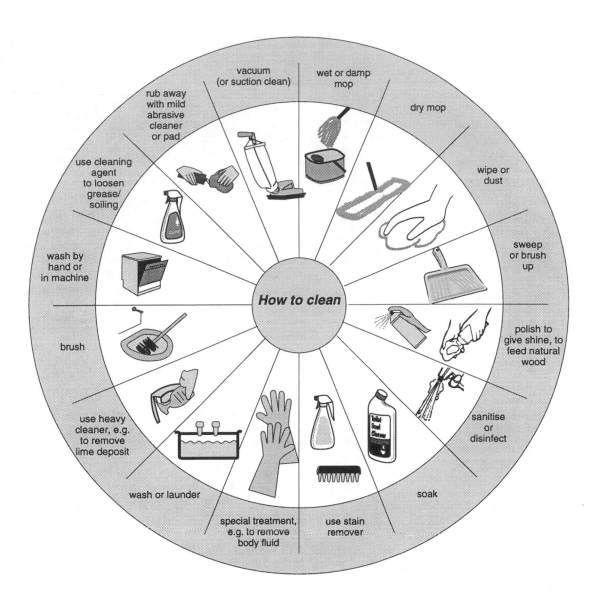

How to clean

- vacuum (or suction clean)
- wet or damp mop
- dry mop
- wipe or dust
- sweep or brush up
- polish to give shine, to feed natural wood
- sanitise or disinfect
- soak
- use stain remover
- special treatment, e.g. to remove body fluid
- wash or launder
- use heavy cleaner, e.g. to remove lime deposit
- brush
- wash by hand or in machine
- use cleaning agent to loosen grease/soiling
- rub away with mild abrasive cleaner or pad

vileda
PROFESSIONAL

Where to use colour-coded cleaning cloths

BLUE
General low risk areas

GREEN
General food and bar use

RED
Sanitary appliances

YELLOW
Wash basins, other wash-room surfaces

Always use two colours within washrooms

Work from the cleanest area toward the dirtiest area

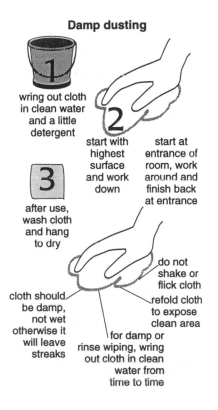

Damp dusting

1 wring out cloth in clean water and a little detergent

2 start with highest surface and work down — start at entrance of room, work around and finish back at entrance

3 after use, wash cloth and hang to dry

do not shake or flick cloth

refold cloth to expose clean area

for damp or rinse wiping, wring out cloth in clean water from time to time

cloth should be damp, not wet otherwise it will leave streaks

what
What does it mean?

Descaler An acid cleaner to remove limescale from taps, toilets bowls, urinals and other bathroom and toilet fittings.

Detergent Substance for removing dirt during cleaning.

Disinfectant Substance for killing bacteria and other microorganisms.

Sanitiser Substance which combines the action of a disinfectant and a detergent.

Toilet bowl cleaner An acid or a bleach or a strong alkaline solution to clean, disinfect and destain toilet bowls.

Why and how you clean **27**

More about vacuum cleaners

Also called suction cleaner and sometimes 'hoover' (the brand name of one of the makers).

Cylinder or canister vacuum cleaners *(left illustration)* have a flexible tube with a wide range of attachments and suck the dirt away.

Some upright vacuum cleaners beat the carpet with a brush or bar to dislodge the dirt, at the same time sucking to remove it *(centre*

illustration). Some models also have a flexible tube and attachments for cleaning crevices and upholstery.

Carpet sweepers *(right illustration)* use a revolving brush (which works when the machine is pushed or pulled), to sweep up crumbs, dry mud that has dropped off shoes and clothes, etc. As they make little noise, they are useful in a room where guests are present – to remove crumbs from the restaurant carpet during service, for example.

Stain removal

The golden rule for treating stains is to act quickly. Try not to leave the stain to set into the fabric.

Check the maker's cleaning instructions. Take non-washable fabrics to a dry cleaner and tell them what the stain is.

If washable:

- test the stain remover on a hidden area: if the colour changes or comes off, consult your supervisor
- try the simplest treatment first: many stains respond to soaking in water and detergent, followed by washing
- don't combine chlorine bleach with any other cleaner or stain removal agent: it may produce toxic gases
- don't over-wet fabrics, use solvent sparingly.

To avoid ring marks when using solvents:

- place the stained area over an absorbent cloth, e.g. towelling
- work from the outside toward the centre, dabbing rather than rubbing.

For other advice on removing stains, see page 60.

Spot or stain removal

Alcohol or food Use soda water. Fizz soda and rub in towards the centre of the spot. If possible, place a towel under affected area.

Blood Blot with concentrated common starch paste and rinse (from the reverse side if possible) with mild soapy water.

Butter Sponge with dry cleaning fluid.

Candle wax Scrape off surface wax. Place brown paper or paper towel over the stain and press with a warm iron. Spot with methylated spirit to remove any colour before washing.

Chewing gum Scrape and sponge with dry cleaning fluid. If the gum is soft, rub with an ice cube placed in a plastic bag (to freeze the gum).

Chocolate Sponge with mild soapy water.

Coffee Sponge with glycerine. If none is available, use warm water.

Cosmetics (the stain is a combination of wax, oil and dye). Dab a waxy stain with white spirit or dry cleaning fluid. Apply glycerine to the dye stain and leave for 1 hour. Soak or wash in a heavy-duty detergent containing oxygen bleach. If the stain remains, treat with hydrogen peroxide.

Egg Scrape and sponge with soapy water.

Glue Sponge with methylated spirits.

Grass and mud Dab with methylated spirit, then rinse in warm water and detergent. Treat with glycerine. Wash in a heavy-duty detergent containing oxygen bleach.

Grease, tar, car oil Sponge with dry cleaning fluid.

Ink Sponge with cold water. If possible, immerse in the water. Or dab with methylated spirit on a cotton wool bud. Or use Stain Devils stain remover.

Lipstick Rub white bread over the area with a firm, gentle motion.

Mud Once dry, brush off and sponge with soapy water (if possible, from the reverse side).

Paint If it is still moist, for oil-based paint dab with white spirit and then wash. For emulsion paint, sponge with cold water and wash immediately. You are unlikely to be able to remove paint which has dried.

Pet stains Use a pet stain remover. Soak and wash fabrics in biological detergent.

Proteins (blood, egg, milk, gravy) Soak in biological detergent and cold water followed by washing with a heavy duty biological detergent.

Tea Sponge with glycerine. If none is available, use warm water.

Unidentifiable stains Treat with glycerine, wash in heavy duty biological detergent and cool water.

Wine As alcohol. If possible, immerse in cold water.

Look after cleaning materials and equipment

Cleaning materials and equipment are high-cost items. Caring for them will help your hotel run efficiently.

Trolley rules

restock before starting

regularly empty and clean

do not overload

avoid blocking corridors

never block fire exits

avoid bumping into walls, furniture, etc.

Prepare what you will need

Before you start the day's duties, or a special task, collect the materials and equipment you need. Your work procedure or job instructions may list what these are. If not, it is a help to make your own list (ask those you work with to help).

Check your room servicing sheet for extra requirements, e.g. special linen for VIP rooms, cots, bed boards.

You may be asked to sign for the master key (or key card) to the rooms you will be servicing.

End of shift duties

Return everything to its proper place so that those next on duty know where to find it.

Take the waste bag from your trolley to a disposal point, and the linen bag to wherever the laundry is collected.

In some hotels, this is the time when trolleys are cleaned down and restocked for the following day.

Report any outstanding problems to your supervisor, and sign back the master key.

Take care of equipment

All equipment must be left clean after use. Wash and rinse cloths, mops and brushes and leave to dry. Damp dust the outside of vacuum cleaners, including the lead. Rewind the lead neatly.

Do not leave brushes of any type resting on their bristle (they get misshapen). Hang up or store upside down.

Do not leave pads or drive plates under floor cleaning machines.

Hang mops up by the handle, or stand handle down in the bucket, so air can circulate around the mop head to dry it.

29

Take care of stock

Pay attention to storage instructions, e.g. THIS SIDE UP and KEEP UPRIGHT.

Do not place heavy items on top of any which might be squashed.

Do not leave stock unattended, unless it is in locked storage. It might be stolen, vandalised or tampered with. Many cleaning materials are dangerous when misused. You know this, others may not.

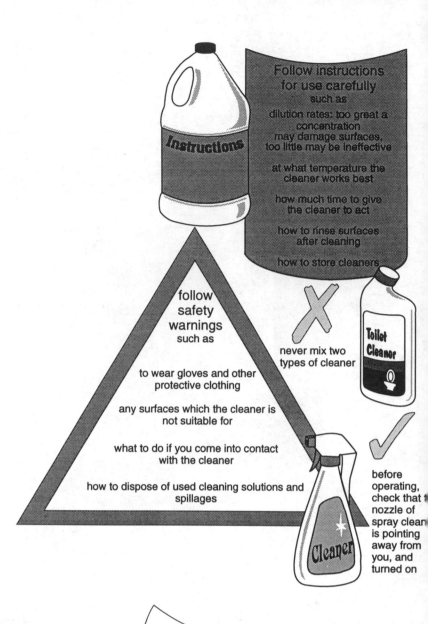

Follow instructions for use carefully such as

dilution rates: too great a concentration may damage surfaces, too little may be ineffective

at what temperature the cleaner works best

how much time to give the cleaner to act

how to rinse surfaces after cleaning

how to store cleaners

follow safety warnings such as

to wear gloves and other protective clothing

any surfaces which the cleaner is not suitable for

what to do if you come into contact with the cleaner

how to dispose of used cleaning solutions and spillages

never mix two types of cleaner

before operating, check that the nozzle of spray cleaner is pointing away from you, and turned on

Toiletries
- ☑ Boxed soaps
- ☑ Shower caps
- ☑ Shampoo sachets
- ☑ Bath gel sachets

Linen
- ☑ Hand towels
- ☑ Bath towels
- ☑ Bath mats

Comfort Inn **Quality Hotel**

Bathroom items
- ☑ Toilet rolls
- ☑ Sanitary bags
- ☑ Tissues

Cleaning agents
- ☑ Toilet cleaner
- ☑ Bath cleaner
- ☑ Air freshener

Your trolley

- Use a service lift to transport trolleys from one floor to another, not the guest lifts.

- Never block a corridor, fire escape route or fire exit with your trolley.

- Keep your trolley within sight at all times to reduce losses.

- Stock your trolley with sufficient linen, cleaning materials and ancillary items for the rooms you will be servicing – additional trips to storage areas should not be necessary. But avoid overloading the trolley, so that it is not safe.

- Your trolley should look presentable and be clean.

Merchandising material
- ☑ Note pads and p
- ☑ Shoe shine cloths
- ☑ Laundry bags/card
- ☑ Compendium conte
- ☑ Dressing table literat
- ☑ Breakfast and minibar order forms
- ☑ Comment forms
- ☑ Do not disturb notices

Hospitality tr items
- ☑ Coffee
- ☑ Decaffeinated cof
- ☑ White/brown suga
- ☑ Sweetener
- ☑ Biscuits
- ☑ Milk cartons
- ☑ Chocolate
- ☑ Tea

Cleaning appliances
- ☑ Clean/dry duster for polishing
- ☑ Clean duster for drying/buffing
- ☑ Soft scourer
- ☑ Sponge/cloth for damp wiping
- ☑ Nail brush
- ☑ Rubber gloves
- ☑ Sponge/cloth for toilet use only
- ☑ Sponge/cloth for other bathroom use only
- ☑ Rubbish sack
- ☑ Bin liners (bedroom bin)

Your trolley
to store and carry what you need
to collect rubbish
to store items for laundry

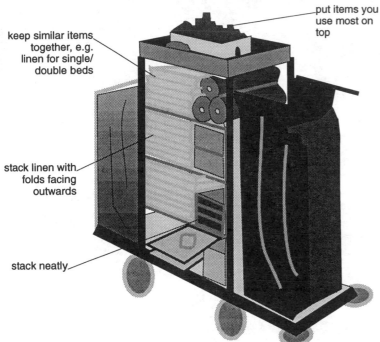

keep similar items together, e.g. linen for single/ double beds

put items you use most on top

stack linen with folds facing outwards

stack neatly

SWALLOW ROYAL HOTEL
BRISTOL

Trolley stock

Item	Qty	Item	Qty
Sheets (jumbo)	10	Guest notepaper & envelopes	20
Sheets (single)	10	Room Service Menu	3
Pillow cases	20	Shoe shine pads	10
Bath robes	4	Sewing cushions	5
Bath mats	10	Directory of services	2
Hand towels	10	Laundry folders	6
Bidet towels	4	Note pads	1
Bath sheets	10	Pencils	2
Face cloths	10	Do Not Disturb notices	3
Sanitary disposal bags	5	Please Service notices	3
Door wedges	2	Breakfast cards	8
Tissues	5	Rubber mats	5
Toilet rolls	10	Tea sachets	40
Body lotion	10	Coffee sachets	40
Soap	20	Sugar sachets	40
Shampoo	20	Hot chocolate	20
Bath gel	20	Biscuits	10

travel inn

Stocking your trolley

- all cleaning materials stored below food items
- clean items stored separately from dirty: clean always above dirty
- all cleaning materials with closing lids
- all food/bedroom consumables sealed

Top shelf is for:

- clean cups, saucers, glasses and teaspoons
- consumable items, soaps, sanitary bags
- DO NOT DISTURB signs, Welcome folders and Welcome folder contents

Middles shelves are for:

- duvet covers, sheets, pillow cases
- towels, bathmats

Bottom shelf is for:

- toilet rolls, space for dirty crockery, carry basket, dust pan and brush
- on the sides will be a white linen bag for reject laundry, tea towels for polishing, a black refuse bag for litter and a long stick duster

The carry basket will contain:

- air freshener, spray polish, all-purpose liquid surface cleaner, toilet cleaner
- floor cloth, J-cloths (blue for basins and baths, green for toilet), kitchen cloth (for polishing chrome and mirrors), cleaning cloth (used damp for other surfaces), a duster and a pair of rubber gloves

Sketchley

Coding system for linen

When linen is folded it can be difficult to tell the difference between double sheets and king size sheets, for example. To distinguish the different sizes, many hotels and linen hire services have a coding system such as:

Single sheets .... blue edging

Double sheets .... red edging

King size sheets .... gold edging

Hand towel .... one header bar

Bath towel ....,,, two header bars

Bath sheet .... three header bars

Vikan

Working position

- Alternate between walking and standing movements.
- Use the large muscle groups (in the arms and legs) as much as possible.
- Avoid tension in fingers and hands over long periods.
- Turn the body by turning the feet.

- Avoid sudden movements that place a burden on the back.
- Be careful in positions involving bending forward and occupying awkward positions.
- Keep the head and shoulders in natural, relaxed positions.
- Handles on equipment should suit the person and the job.

St. David's Park Hotel Golf Club

Maintenance procedure

- Report emergency maintenance needs (including failed light bulbs) immediately by telephone to the housekeeper or duty manager.
- Report other maintenance needs by recording details in the MAINTENANCE BOOK which you will find in the housekeeper's office or reception according to the time of day:

  7 a.m. to 4 p.m.: housekeeper
  4 p.m. to 7 p.m.: reception

- Emergency needs must also be reported in the book as soon as possible: write PHONED THROUGH by the entry.

Using a vacuum cleaner

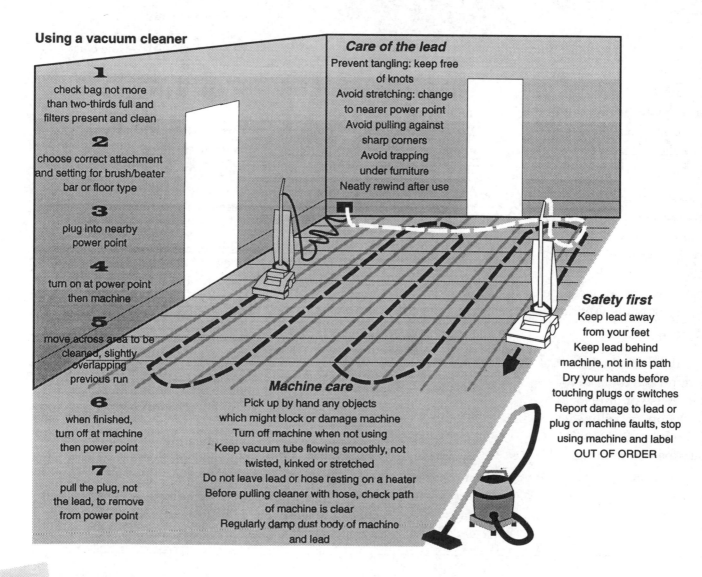

1 check bag not more than two-thirds full and filters present and clean

2 choose correct attachment and setting for brush/beater bar or floor type

3 plug into nearby power point

4 turn on at power point then machine

5 move across area to be cleaned, slightly overlapping previous run

6 when finished, turn off at machine then power point

7 pull the plug, not the lead, to remove from power point

Care of the lead
Prevent tangling: keep free of knots
Avoid stretching: change to nearer power point
Avoid pulling against sharp corners
Avoid trapping under furniture
Neatly rewind after use

Machine care
Pick up by hand any objects which might block or damage machine
Turn off machine when not using
Keep vacuum tube flowing smoothly, not twisted, kinked or stretched
Do not leave lead or hose resting on a heater
Before pulling cleaner with hose, check path of machine is clear
Regularly damp dust body of machine and lead

Safety first
Keep lead away from your feet
Keep lead behind machine, not in its path
Dry your hands before touching plugs or switches
Report damage to lead or plug or machine faults, stop using machine and label OUT OF ORDER

Setting about your work

You may have detailed instructions, with the order for doing tasks. Even so, it is useful to think for a moment and plan the best way to go about your work. Here are some guidelines.

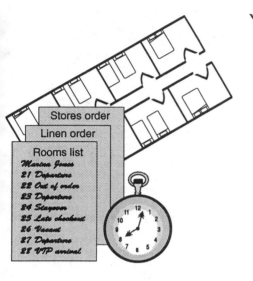

Logical order

Think ahead. For example, before you begin on the bathroom, check you have the cleaning agents, cloths, gloves and other items you need.

Do heavy cleaning tasks and any which create dust first.

Start processes like putting disinfectant in the toilet, in good time so they can be working while you do other tasks.

For the final check, work around the room in a clockwise or anticlockwise direction, or follow a checklist. Otherwise, it is easy to overlook something.

Time and energy

Make each journey count. For example, use one trip to take soiled linen to the trolley and return with clean linen.

Finish one task before you start the next. Switching unnecessarily from one task to another means you take longer than you should and use more physical and mental energy. You are more likely to forget to do things.

Pace yourself. If you spend too much time and energy on one task, you may not be able to do other tasks properly. Rushing from one room to another may seem impressive, but will not get things done quicker than a colleague who works at a steady pace.

Conserve resources

Don't use more than you have to of cleaning materials, and use them correctly. For example, spraying a lot of polish on a surface is a safety risk, makes it difficult to remove, costs extra money and does not do a better job. Leaving the hot water running in the bath while you clean the basin, wastes energy and water.

Switch off lights when you leave the room (unless guests are in the room).

Turn heating down or off and close or open windows, as instructed.

Do your part to help protect the environment

DiverseyLever

Work safely

Remind yourself of what you read in earlier sections of this book on safety, security and hygiene.

A tap left dripping
in the bathroom
can waste up to
a full bath of water
in a day

With thanks to Going for Green, the national environmental awareness campaign. For a free copy of the Green Code, phone 0345 002100.

Follow instructions

A lot goes into creating the standards the guests at your hotel expect, in a way which enables the hotel to operate as a successful business. Play your part by following instructions on what should be done and how.

Small details, like where the guest soap is left in the bathroom and the arrangement of sachets of tea, coffee, sugar etc. on the drink-making tray, are part of the impression guests take away with them. If your hotel belongs to a group or chain, such details will be standard in all the bedrooms.

Question time

1 What preparations should you make before servicing a room?
2 What items should you have on your trolley?
3 Why do we ventilate the room and when should this be done?
4 Why do we leave the toilet cleaner in to soak?
5 What should we check for during the bed-making process?
6 How should we handle soiled linen?
7 Why do we wear rubber gloves and what are the benefits of colour coding them?
8 What do we mean by sanitise?
9 Why do we apply the cleaner or polish to the cloth and not the surface?
10 Why do we use a different cloth for each cleaner?
11 Why is it sensible to use colour-coded cloths?
12 Why should we check for lost property?

Know what order to work in

Know your workplace methods / *Know what to do when* / *Know what to do next*

1 open the windows and curtains	2 turn the lights on, heating off	3 strip the beds	4 check used linen for heavy stains, soiling, damage
6 check for guest belongings left behind	7 report high value items left by guests	8 clear rubbish	9 remove soiled linen
10 remove drinks equipment, bathroom glasses etc.	10 collect linen, remake beds	11 clean bathroom	12 clean bedroom surfaces and fittings
13 replenish supplies	14 record any faults	15 vacuum floors	16 check final appearance, turn down heating

Answer time

(1) Collect everything you need, including cleaning materials and equipment, linen and guest supplies. (2) Cleaning materials, clean linen, guest supplies, waste bags and other items as used in your hotel. (3) So the room smells pleasant and fresh when first tasks on entering the room. It is not necessary to open sealed windows in air-conditioned rooms. (4) To give it time to act. Always follow instructions. (5) Anything the guest may have left behind, including used tissues, etc. which should not be mixed up with the laundry. (6) Carefully, so you do not expose yourself to risk of infection. Soiled linen should be placed in the linen bag or linen chute, not on the floor. (7) To protect yourself from infection and contact with cleaners which may harm your skin. Colour-coded gloves reduce the risk of spreading bacteria to another surface. (8) To destroy harmful bacteria. (9) Applying the cleaner to the cloth helps spread it evenly, and avoids using too much. But check instructions for the products you are using. (10) To avoid mixing different cleaners (which can produce harmful chemical reactions). (11) See answer 7 for colour-coded gloves. (12) So that it can be returned to the owners with minimum delay. The next guests in the room will get a poor impression of housekeeping standards at the hotel if they discover items that should have been found when the room was serviced.

with thanks to Liz Smith-Mills, DiverseyLever

Entering a guest room

You will be given a list or told which guest rooms have to be serviced, and whether they are departures, stayovers, VIPs, day lets, late departures, to be cleared for redecoration, etc.

DO NOT DISTURB

Respect the guest's wishes. Leave the cleaning of the room until the notice has been removed.

If the notice is still in place on a departure room after the check-out time, tell your supervisor.

Also tell your supervisor if a guest has:
- double locked the door, and does not respond to your knocking
- told you not to service the room

Courtesy first!

Never assume the room is vacant, even if a PLEASE SERVICE sign is hanging on the door, or you have been told the guests have departed.

Check your list for guests who have hearing or sight impairments, so that you can be careful to warn them of your presence.

1 Knock and wait

Knock clearly to alert anyone in the room. Allow 15 to 30 seconds for a response.

2 Knock again and wait

Open the door slightly and knock again, saying in a clear voice 'housekeeping' or 'may I service your room?' or the standard greeting used in your hotel.

3 Enter the room

If you get no reply after 15 to 30 seconds and hear no sounds suggesting that someone is in the room, open the door fully and enter.

If the room is dark, turn the light on before entering.

Rooms list for
Ann Lloyd

21 Departure
22 Out of order
23 Departure
24 Stayover
25 Late checkout
26 Vacant
27 Departu
28 VIP arri

4 Proceed with care

Check no one is asleep or using the bathroom and did not hear you knock. If the bathroom door is shut, knock first.

The noise of a radio or TV does not necessarily mean a guest is in the room, but it might have drowned out the sound of your knocking.

In this situation:

- announce yourself again after you have fully opened the door

- proceed carefully until you are sure the room is vacant.

What to do

Do Not Disturb (DNB) sign: note on section sheet with time. If occupied, contact the guest room via the housekeeper at 2 p.m. If a departure, check departure time with reception. Unless special arrangements have been agreed, contact the guest room via the housekeeper at 12 noon.

Please Service sign: give these priority. If many rooms are requesting service, contact the housekeeper. If possible, extra help will be arranged.

VIP rooms: always service these rooms first, unless you already know when the guests would like their room serviced.

The Gleneagles Hotel

When the guest is in the room

Apologise for troubling the guest, and ask when it would be convenient for you to return to clean the room.

If the guest is asleep, leave the room quietly. If you turned the light on, turn it off again.

If you hear sounds indicating the guest is in the bathroom and probably didn't hear you, leave the room quietly. If the guest can hear you from the bathroom, apologise and say that you will return later.

The Gleneagles Hotel

Entering a guest room

Check for any sign on the door, a light underneath, voices or sound of TV or radio or any movement. This will let you know if a guest is likely to be in the room.

Knock with your knuckle three times, announce 'Good morning, housekeeping' and listen. Do not use your keys or any other metal object to knock on the door, as this damages the paintwork/door finish.

If there is no response within five seconds, knock again three times, put your key in the lock, open the door and this time use the guest's name, e.g. Good morning Mr Smith, housekeeping'.

If the guest is not in, bring in your cleaning materials, ready to commence the room servicing.

If guest is in the room or bathroom, apologise for the interruption, and ask politely, using the guest's name, 'When would you like your room serviced, Mr Smith?'

Indicating that you're in a guest room

Make it clear that you are in the room servicing it:

- to warn guests who return to their room of your presence

- as a security measure, so that people know the reason the room is open

- to help colleagues find you, and if there is a fire or security alert, check that you have responded.

Different hotels have their own preferred method:

- *trolley left in the corridor outside the open guest room door.* This discourages passers-by from entering the room on the chance they can steal something. There is a risk of items being removed from the trolley – children might do this, and come to harm by misusing cleaning substances

- *door wedged open.* Do this with a proper wedge, not soiled linen, a chair or other furniture. There is a risk that someone could slip into the room without you realising, giving you a fright or putting you at risk

- *hanging a sign* ROOM BEING SERVICED *and, usually, leaving the door closed.* The trolley is pushed into the room, if practical.

---

what
What does it mean?

A&D list Numbers and names of guests arriving or departing on the day.

Back of house Non-guest areas of the hotel, e.g. store rooms, kitchen, laundry.

Check-out time Latest time for guests to vacate rooms. Guests who have not done so might be required to pay an extra charge, depending on hotel policy.

CIP Commercially Important Person: alternative term to VIP.

Day let Room is in use during the day, e.g. for a meeting. Servicing must wait until the room has been vacated or the following day.

Departure The guest is checking out. Most hotels have a time by which guests must vacate their rooms (e.g. 11 a.m.), although many leave earlier.

DM Duty manager: the person in charge of the hotel, e.g. in the evenings/overnight when the general manager is off duty.

Front of house Areas of the hotel available for guest use.

Late departure or **Late check-out** Guest has arranged to leave late.

No service A guest staying over has asked for the room not to be serviced, and to be undisturbed.

Out of service The room cannot be let for some reason, e.g. redecoration.

Rooms off dirty Rooms which cannot, for the present, be serviced, e.g. because guests have departed late, or staff shortages.

Slept out The state of the bed and the room suggest the guest has been elsewhere overnight.

Stayover The guest is staying another night.

Vacant The room was unoccupied, so does not need cleaning.

VIP Very Important Person, someone the hotel wants to have extra special service.

with thanks to Liz Smith-Mills

Stages to servicing a guest room

You will be shown the way to service the guest rooms in your hotel. What follows is general guidance and examples of particular hotels' methods.

Prepare

It doesn't make sense to clean something if a later task will create more dust or dirt. So it is usual to begin by removing rubbish and the items which are cleaned elsewhere, e.g. cups, saucers, towels and bed linen. This is why stripping the bed is one of the first tasks. Another reason is that stripping the bed creates and moves dust.

To give the room time to air, open the curtains and windows as soon as possible. This is not usually necessary in air-conditioned rooms.

If there is not good natural light coming into the room from the windows, turn the main lights on. This helps you see what you are cleaning.

Bedroom control sheet

Check the bedroom control sheet which identifies your allocated rooms:

- occupied (stayovers) or departures
- how many guests are resident in each room, e.g. doubles at single occupancy
- stayover rooms which require a linen change
- any special periodic cleaning which has to be carried out, e.g. high level dusting.

Make a note of any lights not working. If you will be cleaning the bulbs, this should be done before they have got hot.

If you are using cleaning substances that need time to act, e.g. in the toilet, deal with these now.

Order to service

1

Heavier cleaning tasks and those which need time to work

2

Any which disturb dust

3

Work around room

4

Finish by vacuuming

Begin with the heavier cleaning tasks and any which disturb dust. Work around the room, so there is less risk of forgetting something. The last task is to vacuum the floor.

Remove waste

Avoid direct contact, as the waste may include sharp objects, used tissues and similar items that are a safety risk. Tip the contents of the bin into your waste sack.

If the bin is lined, lift out the liner by its sides, twist it shut and drop it into the waste sack.

If the bin is very full, you may have to remove some items individually (wear gloves) before you can pick the bin up. Otherwise, there is a risk that rubbish will fall on to the floor.

Clean the inside and outside of the bin. Place a new lining bag (where one is used) in the bin, with the top folded over the rim of the bin.

Take care of guests' belongings

Tidy any guests' belongings which have been dropped on the floor, left lying on a bed that you need to make, or on a surface that needs cleaning. Use your judgement on how much tidying to do: guests do not want their belongings tampered with, but some are so untidy, even with their used underwear, that you have little choice. Your supervisor will advise.

Carefully collect any belongings left by departed guests (see page 24 for dealing with lost property).

Call your supervisor if you find valuables or money (unless it is only loose change) left in the room. The guest can then be advised to use the safekeeping facilities, and you are protected from accusations of theft.

Make the bed

As you strip the bed, look out for damage: tears, burn marks, stains, frayed stitching, etc. Avoid direct contact with any damp or wet patches (for hygiene and safety reasons, see page 7). Stained mattress covers should be replaced with clean ones.

Some guests remake the bed. Nevertheless, do check that everything is in order – a neat bedspread may disguise an untidy bed.

If one bed appears not to have been used in a twin room, check it anyway. Even if the room has been let for single occupancy, the guest may have lain or sat on the second bed or put heavy luggage on it, creasing the linen. If the beds are wide ones, two guests may have used one only and left the other bed in perfect condition.

Your hotel may have a scheme for recycling used soap, newspapers, bottles, drink cans, etc. You may have different containers or bags for each type, or one for all recycled items and another for waste.

Lost property
Handed in promptly
Where found
When found

Valuables
Supervisor or
manager
told immediately

Room servicing steps

Clear all rubbish.
Put cups and glasses to soak in steriliser.
After flushing, put toilet renovator into loo.
Clear bathroom of all dirty linen.
Check to see what is missing, soap, etc.
Bring in towels, etc. and place correctly.
Fold toilet paper, arrange tissues.

STEP 1

Service the bathroom

The size and fittings of en-suite bathrooms vary greatly, and so does the time taken to clean them. Probably the most difficult – fortunately not common – are those with huge sunken baths in black enamel: the dark colour means any mark at all shows, yet because of the size you have to get in the bath to reach the far side. Crawling your way out the bath on a bath mat may be the only way to avoid touching a surface once polished!

A simpler routine is described in Section 13. Attention to detail and taking trouble over the final appearance of the bathroom shows your guests that the standards of hygiene and cleaning are what they should be.

To avoid spreading bacteria, cloths or brushes used to clean the toilet should not be put to any other use. A colour-coding system makes this rule easier to follow.

Service the bedroom

The routine is less time-consuming when the room is a stayover. For example, you don't have to clean the inside of drawers, since they may contain guest belongings. Some tasks (e.g. washing windows) may be done on a rota basis, perhaps every month, or left to contractors.

Even though you are following a routine, and you only have limited time to spend on each room, avoid switching to auto pilot. Give each room and each task your individual attention. Hotel guests are individuals, and some will leave things unintentionally or deliberately where you won't find them if you take short cuts: under the bed, behind the cushion on a chair, at the back of the wardrobe shelf, dropped into the bottom of the unit of drawers, and so forth.

Replenish supplies

Again, having a system helps. Until you can remember it accurately, refer to the checklist detailing what must be left in the particular room you are servicing. Quantities depend on how many people might occupy the room. More expensive rooms usually have a more luxurious range of complimentary products.

Check complimentary items remaining from the previous time the room was serviced. Shampoo in a non-see-through plastic screw-top container may have been partly used and the top replaced neatly, or refilled with water. In the drinks caddy there may be opened sachets, carefully kept to make another weak coffee, for example.

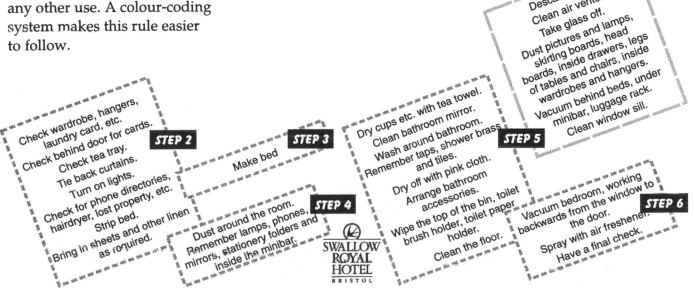

STEP 2
Check wardrobe, hangers, laundry card, etc.
Check behind door for cards.
Check tea tray.
Tie back curtains.
Turn on lights.
Check for phone directories, hairdryer, lost property, etc.
Strip bed.
Bring in sheets and other linen as required.

STEP 3
Make bed

STEP 4
Dust around the room. Remember lamps, phones, mirrors, stationery folders and inside the minibar.

SWALLOW ROYAL HOTEL BRISTOL

STEP 5
Dry cups etc. with tea towel.
Clean bathroom mirror.
Wash around bathroom.
Remember taps, shower brass and tiles.
Dry off with pink cloth.
Arrange bathroom accessories.
Wipe the top of the bin, toilet brush holder, toilet paper holder.
Clean the floor.

WEEKLY
Descale kettle.
Clean air vents.
Take glass off.
Dust pictures and lamps, skirting boards, head boards, inside drawers, legs of tables and chairs, inside wardrobes and hangers.
Vacuum behind beds, under minibar, luggage rack.
Clean window sill.

STEP 6
Vacuum bedroom, working backwards from the window to the door.
Spray with air freshener.
Have a final check.

Final check

This is the time to find the canister of spray polish you forgot behind the curtains, or spot the smear left on the mirror. Now, or at some earlier stage, check that each light and electrical appliance is working, the TV is tuned correctly, and the batteries in the remote control have not lost their strength.

You may have a checklist to follow, which itemises everything that must be examined. Not using this properly means you will probably have to go back to the room later, to put right the problems your supervisor has found.

When you have finished in the room, everything should meet the standard your guests and your employer expect.

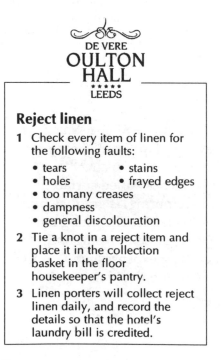

Reject linen

1 Check every item of linen for the following faults:
   - tears
   - holes
   - too many creases
   - dampness
   - general discolouration
   - stains
   - frayed edges

2 Tie a knot in a reject item and place it in the collection basket in the floor housekeeper's pantry.

3 Linen porters will collect reject linen daily, and record the details so that the hotel's laundry bill is credited.

Know what to report

Know what to do about — Know what to report

wet clothes dripping on floor	valuables left in room	guest comes into room you are cleaning	flooded bathroom floor
unpleasant smell in room	no sign of room being used by guest	burn on the blanket, sheet or duvet	wet clothes left on electric heater
you find guest in compromising situation	damage to furniture or fittings	room let as single appears to have two guests	guest has smoked in no-smoking room
missing hotel property	loose change left by guest on table or elsewhere	room occupied by heavy smoker	stain on carpet, furniture or bedding

Know what to do about

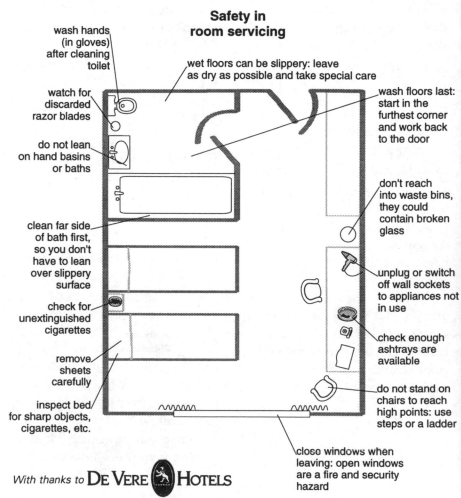

Safety in room servicing

wash hands (in gloves) after cleaning toilet

watch for discarded razor blades

do not lean on hand basins or baths

clean far side of bath first, so you don't have to lean over slippery surface

check for unextinguished cigarettes

remove sheets carefully

inspect bed for sharp objects, cigarettes, etc.

wet floors can be slippery: leave as dry as possible and take special care

wash floors last: start in the furthest corner and work back to the door

don't reach into waste bins, they could contain broken glass

unplug or switch off wall sockets to appliances not in use

check enough ashtrays are available

do not stand on chairs to reach high points: use steps or a ladder

close windows when leaving: open windows are a fire and security hazard

With thanks to DE VERE HOTELS

Service the bathroom

More often than not, you find the bathroom untidy. As a professional you deal with this. You get on with the job of turning chaos into order, to leave everything clean and hygienic.

Combat bacteria

The dirt from people's bodies, faeces, urine and other body fluids are a rich source of bacteria. The warm, moist conditions in bathrooms are ideal for bacteria to multiply. Thorough cleaning, including use of the correct cleaning materials, prevents a dangerous build up of bacteria, and the bacteria from spreading.

Smells, blocked drains and damage to surfaces and fittings can also occur through poor cleaning and maintenance.

Control bacteria

The cloths and brushes you use in bathrooms must be kept for that purpose only. There should be another cloth and brush used only for the toilet.

Colour-coded cloths make this rule easier to follow, e.g. red for toilets, blue for other bathroom fittings. When each en-suite bathroom has its own toilet brush (the safer, more practical arrangement), do not use that brush elsewhere.

If you have to clean up blood, faeces, urine, vomit, semen or any other body fluids from elsewhere, take particular care. Follow the safe cleaning and disposal procedures laid down by your employer for such tasks.

Care for fixtures and fittings

Most baths, basins, toilets and other sanitary fittings are made of durable, easy-to-clean materials. Nevertheless, dropping a heavy or sharp object is likely to damage the surface. Plastic baths and basins scratch readily.

Using the wrong cleaning material can damage any type of surface – the effect (scratches, pitted surface, discolouring) is gradual, but irreversible. The fitting must be replaced or resurfaced, causing expense and disruption.

Service an en-suite bathroom

Removing the rubbish and soiled linen is usually one of the first tasks, part of the routine for preparing the bedroom and bathroom for cleaning (see Section 12).

Clean the toilet

With some toilet cleaners, steps 1 to 4 are done in advance to allow time for disinfection and/or descaling.

1 Flush the toilet.

2 Lift the toilet cover and seat.

3 Using a pumping motion with the toilet brush, get as much water as possible out of the toilet bowl. This exposes the water line for cleaning.

4 Apply toilet cleaner all round the inside of the pan (including the flushing rim). Wet the toilet brush in the toilet bowl, then scrub the inside of the bowl thoroughly, especially the water line and flushing rim.

5 Flush the toilet. Rinse the toilet brush under the clean running water.

6 Hold the toilet brush over the bowl for a few moments to drain, then place it back in the holder.

7 Apply some cleaner (usually the same one you use for other bathroom fittings) to your cloth, and damp wipe the cistern, handle, pipes, toilet brush holder, outside of toilet pan, top and sides of the flushing rim, both sides of the toilet seat and cover as well as the hinge or fitting that holds it in place.

8 With a dry cloth, polish both sides of the seat and lid, the toilet handle and any other external surfaces that look smeary.

9 Lower the toilet seat and close the lid. Some hotels wrap a special paper band around the toilet seat to show it has been sanitised.

STANDARDS CHECK

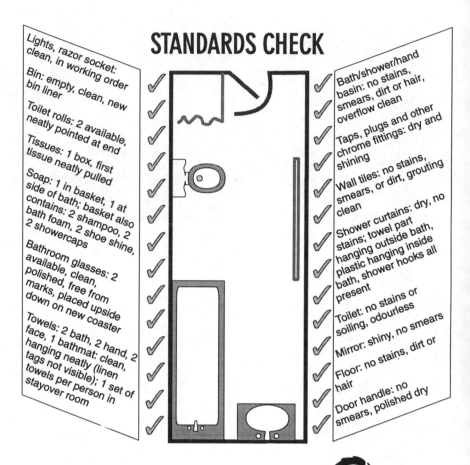

Lights, razor socket: clean, in working order

Bin: empty, clean, new bin liner

Toilet rolls: 2 available, neatly pointed at end

Tissues: 1 box, first tissue neatly pulled

Soap: 1 in basket, 1 at side of bath; basket also contains: 2 shampoo, 2 bath foam, 2 shoe shine, 2 showercaps

Bathroom glasses: 2 available, clean, polished, free from marks, placed upside down on new coaster

Towels: 2 bath, 2 hand, 2 face, 1 bathmat: clean, hanging neatly (linen tags not visible); 1 set of towels per person in stayover room

Bath/shower/hand basin: no stains, smears, dirt or hair, overflow clean

Taps, plugs and other chrome fittings: dry and shining

Wall tiles: no stains, smears, or dirt, grouting clean

Shower curtains: dry, no stains; towel part hanging outside bath, plastic hanging inside bath, shower hooks all present

Toilet: no stains or soiling, odourless

Mirror: shiny, no smears

Floor: no stains, dirt or hair

Door handle: no smears, polished dry

DiverseyLever
With thanks to Liz Smith-Mills

1 Flush toilet.

2 Squirt around inside of bowl to rim.

3 Leave for 10 minutes, then flush.

Some toilet cleaners require time to do their work. If so, begin the process before any other tasks.

Leave combined shower/bath taps on bath setting

... so that guests do not have an unintentional shower!

Clean the wash hand basin

1 Remove soap or, if it is to be used again, put aside while you clean the basin.

2 Move personal property to a convenient place for the guest, or to one side to return when you have finished. Handle razors and razor blades with care so as not to cut yourself.

3 Rinse the basin to dislodge loose dirt and hair. Remove and throw away any waste which has collected in the plug hole (you may have tweezers to do this).

4 Partly fill the basin with warm water (sufficient to rinse your cloth). This is less wasteful than running a tap all the time, with the plug out.

5 Apply cleaner to your damp cleaning cloth. Clean (and if necessary, rinse) outside and underneath the basin, water supply and waste pipes and the pedestal. Clean the rim of the basin, splash back and taps.

6 Empty the water. Clean the inside of the basin, plug and chain.

7 With a dry cloth, shine the taps and polish any smeary surfaces.

Special procedures

Use a stiff brush to clean the insides of the basin overflow hole.

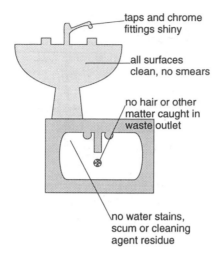

taps and chrome fittings shiny

all surfaces clean, no smears

no hair or other matter caught in waste outlet

no water stains, scum or cleaning agent residue

Clean the bidet

Follow the steps for cleaning a wash hand basin.

Clean the bath

1 Wipe all surfaces inside, outside and around the bath with your cloth and cleaner, and if necessary rinse. Run a little water from the tap when you need to rinse your cloth. It is wasteful to leave the tap running.

2 Remove hair and anything else caught in the plug hole. Check the overflow is clean.

3 Shine the taps and other metal fittings.

To clean low surfaces, bend your knees not your back. This reduces the strain on your back. Or kneel on the floor.

Clean the shower

1 Partly fill your bucket with warm water to rinse out your cloth while cleaning the shower. Or use a nearby basin (which you have not yet cleaned).

2 Using your cloth and cleaner, wipe the shower head, pipes, soap holder, taps, the walls and both sides of the door or curtain and rail to the shower cubicle. Clean the ceiling of enclosed cubicles.

3 Check the shower head has no blocked holes. Depending on the type, report it to maintenance, or remove the head and soak it.

4 Clean the shower floor and surrounding rim or step. Remove any waste caught in the plug hole.

Special procedures

For showers with sliding doors, clean the running track with a brush.

Shower curtains: wipe all over with a cleaning solution and sponge. If possible, press the curtain up against the wall so you have a firm surface to rub against. If the curtain smells, or has got stained or damaged, replace.

To reduce the risk of Legionnaires' disease, shower heads must be regularly dismantled for thorough cleaning and disinfecting.

Clean the walls

Panels or tiling around basins and baths should be cleaned at the same time as the fittings. Cleaning of other wall areas and ventilation or fan vents may form part of a special routine, e.g. monthly, or be done by contractors.

Special procedures

To remove dust, lint and cobwebs from the ceiling, use a feather duster or dry vacuum cleaner with a suitable tool and reach.

To clean fan inlets and air vents (which in the bathroom tend to collect fluff), use a damp cloth or sponge. Turn the fan off first at the isolating switch. A small broom or dry brush may be suitable for air vents in rooms where the air does not get steamy.

Never climb on the toilet or the bath edge to reach high surfaces: use steps, a long-handled brush or reach pole.

Replenish supplies

Replace towels, bathmats and other linen items (e.g. face cloths) as appropriate for the room. In some hotels, towels are folded in a particular way so that you can tell which have not been used and can be left for the next guest.

In many hotels, all towels are replaced even if the guests are staying another night. Other-wise used towels in stayover rooms are left neatly folded, unless they are heavily soiled or stained or very damp.

As necessary, replace toilet rolls, tissues, soap and complimentary products (e.g. shampoo, bath foam). It is usual to leave a second toilet roll, unless the dispenser holds an extra-long roll. Some hotels also provide a hard toilet paper.

To discourage guests from flushing sanitary towels down the toilet (which can lead to a blockage), special disposal bags, or other suitable facilities may be provided.

Drinking glasses should be left spotlessly clean (after washing in a sanitising liquid). In some hotels, they are enclosed in a plastic bag.

Clean the floor

This is done last, when there is no further need to walk over the floor. Carpeted floors are vacuumed. Hard floors are mopped or wiped over with a floor cloth. This is done twice, first with the cleaning solution, and then with rinsing water to pick up the soiled solution. Mops or cloths should be half-wrung the first time to give enough solution to clean the surface without over-wetting the floor.

To avoid walking over wet surfaces, start at the furthest corner and work back to the door.

Some finishing touches

shiny mirrors, taps and other surfaces, free of smears

towels hanging or folded neatly

soap, shampoo, other complimentary products and spare toilet roll in place

toilet roll placed so that loose end is away from wall

end of toilet roll hanging neatly, not too long nor roughly torn

box of tissues ready for use, first tissue sticking neatly out of box

in some hotels, the end of the toilet roll and tissues are folded to a point

guest belongings neatly arranged

Service the bedroom

With not much time to service each room, it's best to keep to a routine, based on workplace procedures, and the training you have been given in your job. What follows is a typical approach.

The main differences in routine

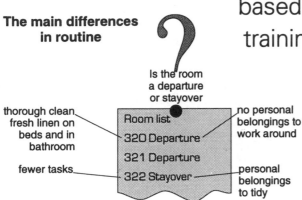

Is the room a departure or stayover

thorough clean, fresh linen on beds and in bathroom

fewer tasks

Room list
320 Departure
321 Departure
322 Stayover

no personal belongings to work around

personal belongings to tidy

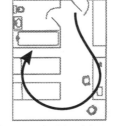

Start at one side of the room and work your way around

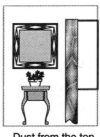

Dust from the top down

Departure rooms

1 Turn the heating down or off, as instructed. Open the windows to air the room. (None of this may be necessary if the heating is controlled automatically, and/or the room is fully air-conditioned.)

2 Empty the waste bins and ashtrays, and collect any rubbish left lying about.

3 Remove china and glassware, room service trays and any other items that are washed elsewhere.

4 Strip and remake the bed(s) (see Section 15). Place the soiled linen in the bag on your trolley, or the linen chute.

5 Clean the wash hand basin (in rooms without their own bathroom), see page 43. Generally, this is the stage when bathrooms of en-suite rooms are cleaned.

6 Starting at a fixed point (e.g. the door or window) work around the room to clean all surfaces and fittings (as set out in your schedule for departure rooms). If you find personal belongings left by guests, put them safely aside, to report and hand in to your supervisor (see page 24).

7 Sanitise guest room china and glasses (or replace with items cleaned elsewhere).

8 Check and replenish guest supplies, e.g. drink sachets, laundry list, minibar, shoe shine cloths.

9 Vacuum throughout the room, including under the beds and furniture. Start at the side of the room furthest from the door, and work your way back to the door. This means you end up with the vacuum cleaner at the door, ready to carry to the next room. It also avoids walking over an area you have just vacuumed. Vacuum in the direction of the pile on thick carpets, to leave an even appearance.

10 Use the upholstery tool to vacuum chairs. In some hotels, this is done at the same time as step 6.

11 Shut windows and readjust heating.

12 Check the room finally: is all as it should be?

13 In some hotels, the vacuuming is done now, when there is no further need to walk over the carpet.

14 Lock the room door. Inform your supervisor/ reception that the room has been serviced.

DE VERE
OULTON
HALL
★★★★★
LEEDS

Checking a minibar

1 Knock on door, greet the guest by name and ask if you may check the minibar.

2 Check the minibar contents against your checklist. Note the quantity of any item missing (presumably consumed by the guest), e.g. '2' against GIN on the list.

3 Tidy the remaining stock: each item in its correct position, labels facing toward the front.

4 Check seals are not broken on bottle tops: do this carefully, since some guests go to considerable trouble to make bottles of spirits look as though they have not been opened (e.g. refilling a whisky with tea). Check products have not reached their best-before or use-by date.

5 Check for cleanliness.

6 Write the room number on the checklist, and its status: O/D (occupied dirty), V/D (vacant dirty) or IN (guest in room).

7 Take completed checklist to the housekeeper's office. Report any minibars not working properly or damaged.

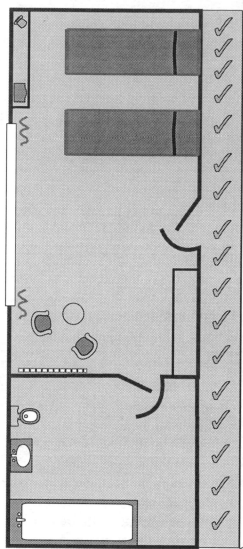

FINAL CHECK

✓ windows closed
✓ heating adjusted
✓ curtains hanging properly
✓ bed spread/bed linen hanging neatly
✓ lamp shades and pictures straight and clean
✓ lights working
✓ TV, radio, kettle, hairdryer, trouser press, etc. working
✓ minibar stocked
✓ no smears on mirrors or polished surfaces
✓ drawers and cupboard doors fully shut
✓ doors free of finger marks
✓ carpet under and around furniture clean
✓ furniture in correct position
✓ guest supplies replenished
✓ no cleaning materials left in room
✓ waste bins and ashtrays empty and clean
✓ items needing repair or special cleaning reported

Room service tips

At the start of the day, make sure you have all your cleaning supplies, linen and towels and your trolley is fully stocked

With a damp cloth wipe inside drawers, wardrobe and all surfaces; in departure rooms, leave drawers and wardrobe open for checking

Use your door wedge to keep the door open: never use linen or furniture

Using hard surface cleaner sanitiser, wipe down all washable surfaces: walls, paintwork, window sills, luggage racks and skirting board

When stripping the bed, place pillows and blankets on a chair, never the floor

If furniture polish is needed, spray on a duster/cloth, never on to surface

DiverseyLever

DiverseyLever

Room Service

Check all lights
Open curtains and windows
Turn radiators down
Remove rubbish

Flush toilet, squirt cleaner around rim and leave

Make beds

Damp dust/polish surfaces

Wash bath and handbasin
Polish taps and chrome
Polish mirrors
Check plug holes and chains

Clean inside toilet, flush
Wash surrounds and seat

Replace guest supplies

Wash bathroom floor
Vacuum bedroom carpet

Final check
Lightly spray with air freshener

Close and lock door

'Stayover' rooms

1 Ventilate the room and remove the rubbish, floor service trays, etc. as for a departure room. Be careful not to treat as rubbish something the guest may want again, e.g. a re-sealed, half-finished container of drink. If a bathroom glass is part-filled with a dental solution, leave it.

2 Sanitise the bedroom china and bathroom glasses.

3 Move or tidy guest belongings as necessary: follow workplace guide-lines and your own judgement of how much tidying to do (see overleaf).

4 Tidy the bed. If the blankets and sheets have been pulled loose, remake the bed. Replace any sheets or pillow cases which have stains (e.g. of blood). In some hotels, beds are remade with clean linen each day, otherwise this is done every 2 to 7 days of a long stay (depending on prices charged/policy).

Non-smoking rooms

A NO SMOKING sticker must be on the corridor side of the door and a NO SMOKING tent card on the dressing table in the room. There should be no ashtrays in the room.

When someone has been smoking in a non-smoking room, it will be necessary to change the bedcovers and blankets. If the curtains have absorbed the smell of smoke, they will also have to be changed.

5 Clean the bathroom. Replace very damp or soiled towels. Bathroom linen will usually be changed with the same frequency as the bed linen.

6 Damp dust tops of tables and units. Polish mirrors and any glass surfaces which are smeared.

7 Top up supplies of soap, drink sachets, etc. Follow hotel policy on whether to replace partly-used soap.

8 Vacuum the floor as required. In some hotels, this will be daily. Other-wise it is done as necessary to remove crumbs, dried mud, powder, granules of coffee, etc., and to restore the pile to the carpet (some footwear leaves noticeable footprints).

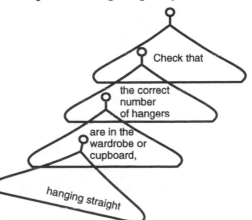

Check that the correct number of hangers are in the wardrobe or cupboard, hanging straight

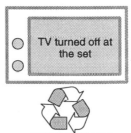

TV turned off at the set

LEAVING TV ON STAND-BY, OPERATED BY THE REMOTE CONTROL, WASTES ENERGY

Deal with guest belongings in a stayover room

In luxury hotels, guests expect their clothes to be put away in cupboards or drawers. There may even be a butler to do this, or a 'personal maid', who also helps prepare clothes required for evening wear, or the next day.

In hotels offering a less personal service, some tidying is necessary and acceptable. So you might:

- move clothes from the bed to the chair, in order to remake the bed

- put in one place shoes left all round the room

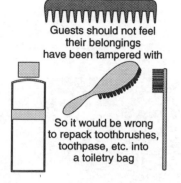

Guests should not feel their belongings have been tampered with

So it would be wrong to repack toothbrushes, toothpase, etc. into a toiletry bag

- pick up an alarm clock or calculator from the floor (where it might get trodden on), and put it on the bedside table

- place on a chair clothes left on the floor (if you put the clothes in a wardrobe, the guest may not look there and forget the item)

- hang wet clothes on the line in the bathroom, if they have been left dripping on the floor, or draped over a heater or furniture. If you take the clothes elsewhere to dry, leave a note to inform the guest.

If night clothes have been left on top or underneath the pillows, replace them there when you have remade the bed.

Service a section of rooms

Sometimes it makes sense to clean a number of rooms at the same time, e.g. clearing up after the departure of a large conference or coach party, and preparing for the next. Working on your own, or as a team with other assistants, you might then:

- remove rubbish from all the rooms

- strip all the beds and remove linen from bathrooms

- remake all beds

- clean each bedroom and bathroom in sequence

- replenish supplies in all rooms

- vacuum all rooms.

The Gleneagles Hotel

Special tasks

Dressing table
- lift off all items and damp wipe
- dry polish glass, turn glass twice weekly
- remove supplies and drawer paper, wipe and replace
- dust legs and drawer fronts so free from finger marks
- ensure handles hang neatly

Bar units
- damp wipe and dry top and shelves (remove contents of bar unit to do this)
- dust sides, low edges and doors, damp wiping and drying sticky finger marks or spillage

TV trolley
- dry dust front, top, screen, back of TV, use damp sponge for any sticky marks, shelf and legs of trolley
- lift TV off trolley weekly, damp wipe and polish glass/wood
- turn over trolley glass once a month

Radiator
- dust daily, brush twice weekly, wash twice monthly
- check for any debris behind radiator
- check radiator is off when turned to 1
- report cold or leaking radiators to housekeeper

Hair dryer
- dust all parts daily
- damp wipe flex weekly, vacuum grill at back of hair dryer weekly

Lights
- chandeliers: use fluffy duster daily on all arms and bulbs
- picture lights: dust and dry daily, re-check position
- globe lights: use fluffy duster daily for bulb and fitting; weekly damp wipe (N.B. light off)
- ceiling lights: house porters to remove, wash and replace four times per year

Make the bed

A well-made bed looks good and is comfortable for guests to sleep in. How this effect is achieved depends on the style of the hotel.

What's what

Bed base

On which the mattress rests. This may be an upholstered, sprung 'divan' base, similar to a mattress but attached to a wooden frame and with feet or castors. Bases of this type have a firm or a soft edge, and some have drawers to provide storage space. Other types of bed base include:

- solid panel of wood
- slats of wood or metal
- wire mesh fixed to a metal or wooden frame
- wire mesh attached to springs.

Divan bases should be vacuumed periodically. Other types of base should be damp dusted or brushed.

Mattress

This needs to be turned every three months or so, to spread the wear and tear. Vacuum periodically (the human skin constantly sheds dead scales in the form of very fine dust).

Valance

If used, this provides a decorative touch and hides the base of the bed. There should be no scuff marks or soiling from contact with shoes, etc. Should be laundered regularly.

Mattress cover

To protect the mattress, requires regularly laundering. Some hotels use waterproof mattress covers. An under-blanket sometimes takes the place of a mattress cover.

Undersheet

Comes between the body of the sleeping guest and the mattress cover or under-blanket. Usually changed at the same time as the top sheet and pillow cases. Fitted sheets have elasticated corners so they pull tight over the mattress. Flat sheets must be tucked in on all sides.

Pillows

Usually two per guest (i.e. four on a double bed). Generally the pillow is covered with an underslip and a pillow case or slip which is changed at the same time as the sheets. The underslip should be checked each time the pillow cases are changed, and replaced with a freshly laundered one if there are any stains.

Top sheet

A flat sheet which comes between the body of the sleeping guest and the blankets. At the pillow end of the bed, the top portion of the sheet is folded back over the blankets (to keep the edge of the blanket away from the guest's face). In hotels which use duvets, there may not be a top sheet (because the duvet cover is changed each time).

Blanket(s) or duvet

To provide warmth. In hot weather, one blanket is usually sufficient, with two or more in cold weather. Some hotels use a different duvet in winter (with a higher tog value), or replace the duvet with a sheet and a light blanket.

Blankets and duvets require cleaning from time to time (some types can be washed, others must be dry cleaned, check the label). Duvet covers should be changed at the same time as the undersheet and pillow slips. In some hotels, a top sheet is used as well as a duvet cover, so that the duvet cover requires less frequent washing.

Bedspread

This covers the whole bed, protecting the bed linen (guests often put suitcases on the bed), and adds to the appearance of the room. The bedspread may be fitted or loose. With some types, the top of the bedspread is folded around the pillows, enclosing them. Some hotels use a quilted bedspread instead of a bedspread and blanket. Bedspreads are not usual with a duvet.

In luxury hotels, house-keeping staff remove the bedspreads in the evening and turn down the blanket and top sheet on one side of the bed (see Section 16).

Scatter cushions

To provide a distinctive touch in more elaborately decorated bedrooms, and for beds which provide seating during the day. Scatter cushions are put aside overnight (as the bed will also have pillows), so the covers only need cleaning from time to time. The pillows of sofa beds are usually kept in a cupboard during the day (covered with clean pillow slips).

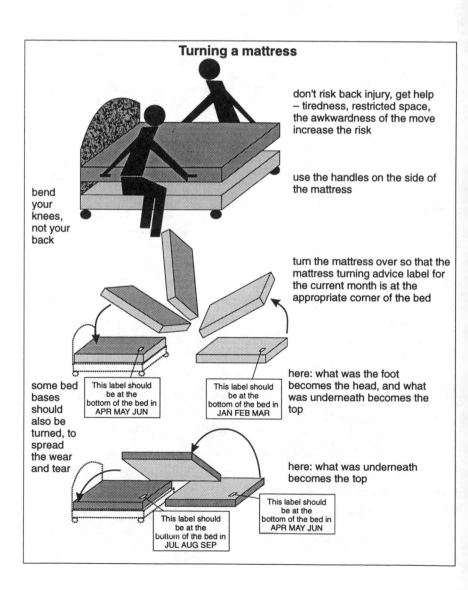

Turning a mattress

don't risk back injury, get help – tiredness, restricted space, the awkwardness of the move increase the risk

bend your knees, not your back

use the handles on the side of the mattress

turn the mattress over so that the mattress turning advice label for the current month is at the appropriate corner of the bed

some bed bases should also be turned, to spread the wear and tear

This label should be at the bottom of the bed in APR MAY JUN

This label should be at the bottom of the bed in JAN FEB MAR

here: what was the foot becomes the head, and what was underneath becomes the top

This label should be at the bottom of the bed in JUL AUG SEP

here: what was underneath becomes the top

This label should be at the bottom of the bed in APR MAY JUN

General points on making beds

Space to work in

If the bed is against the wall, pull it away so that you can get access to both sides.

Surprises: pleasant and unpleasant

When stripping the bed, watch out for tissues, jewellery, clothing, teddy bears, hot water bottles and any other items that might have been left in the bed.

Hygiene and safety

Avoid flapping the linen as this will scatter dust and bacteria. Fold or bundle sheets from the outer corners to the centre of the bed (see illustration on page 53).

Place soiled linen directly into your laundry bag. Do not leave it on the bedroom or corridor floor or use it to prop open a door – linen left in this way gives a poor impression to guests, is a fire hazard and may cause someone to trip.

Never place blankets or clean linen on the floor or any other surface where they may pick up dirt or fluff.

To put a clean slip on the pillow, place the pillow and

To tuck in, bend your knees not your back.

slip on the bed. It may help to fold the pillow in two, lengthways, to get it into the slip. Open the pillow out once it is fully inside the slip. It is unhygienic to tuck the pillow under your chin while you are putting on a clean slip.

Right way up

If sheets have a top and bottom side, the top (smoother) side should be in contact with the guest's body. This means placing the bottom sheet the right way up and the top sheet the wrong side up. The hem of the top sheet, visible when folded over the blanket, should always be the correct way up.

If sheets have a narrow hem at one end and a wide hem at the other, the wide hem should be at the head of the bed.

The overhang of sheets and blankets on each side of the bed should be the same.

The open end of pillow slips should face the direction they are least likely to be seen. The tucked-in side should be nearer to the mattress. On a double bed, the open end of pillow slips should face the centre of the bed (or the same direction for patterned slips).

Any pattern or design on sheets, pillow slips and duvet covers should face the right way round, viewed from the foot of the bed.

what
WHAT DOES IT MEAN?

Down The soft, very fine feathers from the breast of fowl (geese or duck are the best quality). Used to stuff pillows, duvets and quilts of the most luxurious quality. A 'down filling' as described on the label can include up to 15% of very small, fluffy feathers. A 'down and feather' filling can have up to 49% of feather. Least expensive of the three types is 'feather and down', with up to 85% feather.

Tog Used to indicate the warmth provided by a duvet. Duvets range between a tog of 8 (lighter, summer use, normally) to 14 (very warm).

Z-bed Bed which folds up when not in use. Often used to provide an extra bed in what is normally a double or twin room, e.g. so a child can sleep with the parents.

Zip and link Two single beds that zip together to form a double bed.

Valances should hang evenly around the bed.

Duvets

Duvets must lie flat inside their cover. The open edge of duvet should be at the foot of the bed.

Any labels on a duvet should lie at the foot of the bed or on the wall side of the bed (or on the side guests are least likely to use to get into the bed).

Allergies

Some guests are allergic to down and feather fillings. Pillows and duvets stuffed with a manufactured product such as hollow fibre or terylene should be available.

Making a bed with blankets

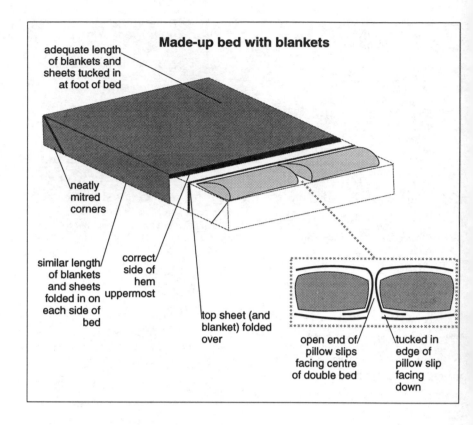

Made-up bed with blankets

adequate length of blankets and sheets tucked in at foot of bed

neatly mitred corners

similar length of blankets and sheets folded in on each side of bed

correct side of hem uppermost

top sheet (and blanket) folded over

open end of pillow slips facing centre of double bed

tucked in edge of pillow slip facing down

Stripping and straightening

1 Strip the bed. As you do so, watch for anything left in the bed (tissues, clothes, etc.) and stains or damage to the linen, blankets, duvet, mattress cover, etc. Place the bed cover, blankets and pillows to one side (e.g. on a chair or another bed). Place the linen for laundering in the bag on your trolley, the laundry chute, or linen bag. Fold up stained or torn linen and put aside for special attention.

2 Straighten the mattress cover or underblanket. Replace with a clean one if stained, damaged or badly creased.

Sheeting

3 Place the bottom sheet on the bed, so that there is a similar length overhanging the top and bottom of the bed. Mitre each corner (see diagram on facing page) of a flat sheet, and tuck in all sides so the sheet is drawn tight across the mattress.

4 Place the top sheet on the bed. To allow for the turn over, the top hem of the sheet should be level with the top of the mattress. Smooth the sheet flat.

The blankets

5 Place the first blanket on the bed. The top of the blanket (this may have an extra wide border) should not be quite as high as the top of the sheet (so that when the sheet is folded over, the wide hem of the sheet lies over the edge of the blanket). (In some hotels, the top of the blanket is not folded over with the sheet. In this case, it should not go as high up the bed.)

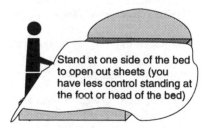

Stand at one side of the bed to open out sheets (you have less control standing at the foot or head of the bed)

6 Place the second blanket (and any others) on the bed in the same way, first checking that each one is lying flat.

Folding and tucking in

7 Fold over a pillow's width or rather less (preferences differ) of the top sheet and blanket(s). The idea is for the guest to be able to get into the bed easily, with enough covering of sheet and blanket at the top of the bed to tuck up warmly. A band of folded-over sheet should be visible once the pillows have been placed on the bed. If the blankets are thick ones, or there are two or more, it is neater not to fold them.

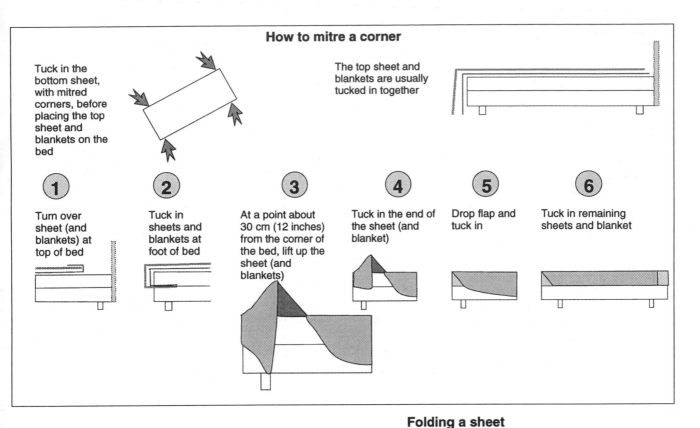

How to mitre a corner

Tuck in the bottom sheet, with mitred corners, before placing the top sheet and blankets on the bed

The top sheet and blankets are usually tucked in together

1 Turn over sheet (and blankets) at top of bed

2 Tuck in sheets and blankets at foot of bed

3 At a point about 30 cm (12 inches) from the corner of the bed, lift up the sheet (and blankets)

4 Tuck in the end of the sheet (and blanket)

5 Drop flap and tuck in

6 Tuck in remaining sheets and blanket

8 Tuck in the sheet and blankets at the foot of the bed.

9 Mitre both corners (of the top sheet and blankets) at the foot of the bed. Tuck in the rest both sides of the bed. (Some hotels leave both sides untucked, or the side of the bed which guests will use to get into the bed.)

Pillow slips and bed cover

10 Put a clean pillow slip on each pillow. Ensure the pillow is enclosed by the flap at the open end of the slip. Position the pillows, neatly plumped up, at the head of the bed.

11 Place the bedspread on the bed. It should lie smoothly.

Folding a sheet
which needs special attention
(e.g. because it is stained)

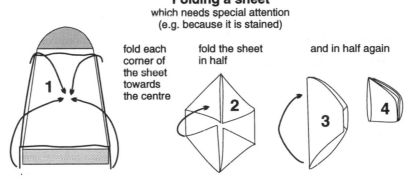

1 fold each corner of the sheet towards the centre

2 fold the sheet in half

3 and in half again

4

The Gleneagles Hotel

Bedmaking tips

Stripping

Removing pillow slips: keep correct side out to assist with the laundering.

Removing bedspread: fold up and across, then place on a chair.

Removing blankets: fold roughly and place on top of bedspread, on chair.

Soiled linen: keep pillow slips separate from sheets for easy counting.

Damaged linen: tie in a big knot and place with soiled linen.

Badly stained or foul linen: place in a different bag from other linen (e.g. one coloured yellow or red), and give to the linen porter separately.

Making

Laying sheets: open out sheet fully, centre fold over centre of bed. Ensure sheet is hanging evenly on both sides, top and foot of mattress. Pull sheet very tight when tucking in.

Placing blankets: unfold blanket across bed, with equal hanging on either side, taking to 23 cm (9 inches) from top edge of mattress.

Placing pillows: open pillow slip, fold pillow in half lengthways and ease into the slip. Smooth into corners of the slip, so the pillow lies neatly with no creases.

Making up a baby's cot

Check the cot is in sound condition and clean. Wheel the cot to a suitable place in the guest's room. If the cot has to be carried, get the help of a colleague. When the guest is in the room, ask where to leave the cot. Avoid blocking the route to the bedroom or bathroom door.

Check the mattress has a clean waterproof cover. If not place a waterproof sheet on top of the underblanket.

Make up the cot with sheets and blankets (of cot size) in the same way as a bed. Only provide a pillow if the parent requests one (because of the danger of the baby suffocating).

Place extra towels in the bathroom, which the parent can use for bathing and changing the baby's clothes.

Providing a bed board

Guests who suffer from back trouble may request a bed board, to provide an extra firm sleeping surface. The board is usually a sheet of plywood or chipboard cut to a suitable size for a single or double bed.

With the help of a colleague, lift the mattress up so the bedding is disturbed as little as possible.

Place the bed board on the base of the bed and lower the mattress.

If the bed board is not as wide as the bed, place it in the centre of a single bed, or on the side of a double bed on which the guest will be sleeping.

Setting up a cot

1 Make up the cot with bottom and top sheets, blankets or quilt, all tucked in, neat and tidy.
2 Place a changing mat on top of the luggage rack.
3 Place an extra bath sheet and hand towel in the bathroom.

Setting up an extra bed

1 Rearrange the furniture in the room:
   – place bed under the window
   – move table and chairs to near the trouser press
   – move the luggage rack to near the dressing table.
2 Make up the bed with one pillow, bottom sheet, duvet and clean duvet cover.
3 Place an extra bath sheet and hand towel in the bathroom.
4 On the tea tray place one extra of each of the following:
   • milk   • cream
   • hot chocolate   • biscuits
   • cup   • saucer
   • teaspoon

Special requests

Bed boards

• Place between the bed base and mattress.
• Corners must not project beyond the edge of the bed base.
• Keep a record of which rooms bed boards are issued to.
• Remove from departure rooms.
• Clean before storing.

Foam pillows for asthmatic and allergy-prone guests

• Keep a record of where they are located.
• Store in plastic covers when not in use.

Water resistant undersheets

• Lay between bottom sheet and mattress.

Disabled guests

• Listen carefully to what the guest tells you about his or her requirements. As requested, explain where everything in the room is to be found.
• Rearrange the furniture to suit the guest. Those with impaired mobility may need to move about in a wheelchair/zimmer frame.
• Do not further reorganise a room occupied by a blind or partially sighted guest, since the guest will expect to find things in the position last used/described.
• Make a note of the room number and duration of stay in case the guest needs further special assistance, or in the event of a fire or other emergency.

Evening 'turndown' service

In hotels providing a high level of personal service, guest rooms are serviced in the evening: the beds turned down (and remade if necessary), even the towels may be replaced.

Enter the room

When there is a DO NOT DISTURB sign on the door, note this on your check sheet/report. Otherwise, knock clearly at the door, and say that you have come to turn the beds down. The guest may say 'no thanks', 'it's not convenient', 'please come back later', etc. Respect these wishes, and make a note of rooms where guests have refused service.

Service the room

The aim is to prepare the room for night-time use. Your tasks may include some or all of the following.

Turn down the bed

Remove bedspreads, fold neatly and place in the cupboard.

Turn back the top sheet and blankets on the side of the bed that the guest is most likely to use. On a double bed, turn down both sides.

Fluff up the pillows.

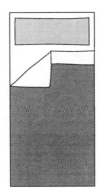

Turn down a single bed on the side that the guest is likely to use

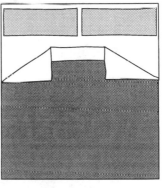

Turn down each side of a double bed which will be occupied by two people

Tidy away

Empty waste bins and ashtrays. Wash and replace bedroom china and glassware. Clear away room service trays.

Generally tidy the room and bathroom: hang towels left on the bath edge or floor, wipe around the basin or bath to remove 'tide' marks, brush and flush the toilet if it has been left unpleasant, etc.

Check there are sufficient supplies of soap, shampoo, bath foam, toilet paper, tissues, drink sachets, etc.

Leave the room ready for the guests' return

Place giveaways on the bedside table or pillow, e.g. chocolates. In some hotels, a bathrobe is folded neatly and placed on the foot of the bed.

Close windows and curtains. Use the pull cord to draw curtains. If there is no pulley system, use the flat palm of your hand to ease the curtains along the rail. Grabbing the edge of the curtains to pull them shut (or open) increases wear and tear.

Leave a bedside or table light on, to welcome guests back into the room.

Turndown service: suites

1 Collect list from evening housekeeper, showing which suites are occupied. Between 6.30 p.m. and 7 p.m. start the turndown service.

2 Knock on door and call 'Good evening, housekeeping'. If there is no reply, knock again and then let yourself into the room. If there is a reply, greet the guest by name and ask if a turndown service is required. If 'No', apologise for bothering the guest and say 'Good night'. If 'Yes', ask when it would be convenient to do it.

3 If the guest has not used the room (e.g. due to arrive later, or there is luggage in the room but no other sign that the guest has been in):
   • turn the bed(s) down
   • close the curtains (but not on a bright summer evening).

4 For occupied rooms:
   • remove any room service trays
   • wash cups, saucers, teapots, glasses, etc. if used
   • replenish tea, coffee, milk, etc.
   • turn bed(s) down
   • close curtains if it is dark outside or the guest has already partly closed them
   • clean toilet if necessary and re-point the toilet paper
   • wipe bath, basin, shower screens, etc. so they are dry
   • polish mirror
   • replenish soap if necessary
   • replace towels if very wet, otherwise refold with the lines facing outward so the person servicing the room the next day knows they have been used
   • wipe bathroom floor
   • ensure all lights are out except bedside lamps
   • ensure door locks when you leave.

The welcoming room

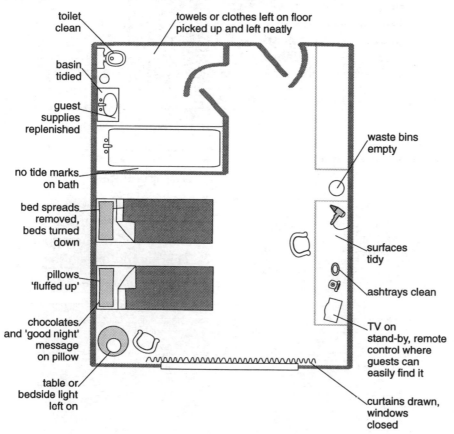

toilet clean

towels or clothes left on floor picked up and left neatly

basin tidied

guest supplies replenished

no tide marks on bath

bed spreads removed, beds turned down

pillows 'fluffed up'

chocolates and 'good night' message on pillow

table or bedside light left on

waste bins empty

surfaces tidy

ashtrays clean

TV on stand-by, remote control where guests can easily find it

curtains drawn, windows closed

Special tasks

You may be asked, for example, to spot clean or shampoo an upholstered chair which has had a drink spilled over it. Some specialist tasks are required to deal with the gradual build up of dirt, for example shampooing carpets. Some may be done by contractors.

Shampoo soft furnishings

This is necessary to remove ingrained dirt and prevent a build-up of dirt, e.g. every 6 months for heavily used furniture. It also gets rid of any pests that have burrowed into the furnishings, e.g. fleas.

Shampooing of furniture may be done by contractors, with special equipment.

Check colour-fastness

If the item has not been shampooed previously, check for colour fastness:

- make up a small quantity of shampoo solution

- moisten a white cloth with the solution and rub over a small area of the item (choose a place which is not likely to be seen)

- after a minute or so, wipe the treated area with a fresh, clean white cloth: if the cloth has picked up colour from the upholstery,

do not proceed. Show your supervisor the results of your test. Some other method of cleaning will probably have to be used.

Remove stains

Heavy stains are unlikely to be removed by the normal shampooing. Depending on the cause of the stain:

- remove it before shampooing (see page 60)

- alternatively, apply a spot remover to the affected area shortly before shampooing. This should loosen the stain.

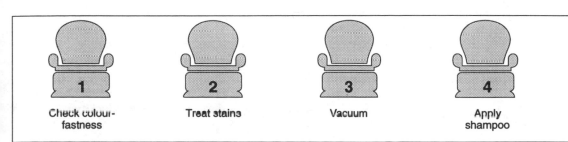

1	2	3	4	5
Check colour-fastness	Treat stains	Vacuum	Apply shampoo	Vacuum

General procedure for shampooing

1 Cover the carpet or floor under the furniture you will be shampooing. Always get help to move heavy furniture.

2 Vacuum clean all the upholstered surfaces. Use a crevice tool to reach down the sides of chairs and couches. Use an upholstery tool for other surfaces, and short sweeping strokes. Pass the suction head over each section at least twice. Overlap each section to make sure you cover the entire surface.

3 Make up the shampoo solution, following instructions. Fill the machine, if used.

4 Work in small sections, using short sweeps with the shampooing head. Do not over-wet the upholstery.

5 When the upholstery is dry, vacuum all surfaces to remove the residue of shampoo and dissolved dirt.

The vacuuming stage is combined if you are using a hot water extraction machine. This either injects the shampoo into the fabric in one mode, and vacuums it out in another mode or does the two operations together.

Do not allow wood or metal objects to rest on wet carpet: separate using pieces of card, foil or plastic.

Polish furniture

General-purpose spray-on furniture polishes are suitable for many surfaces. Spray a little on your polishing cloth and rub the furniture well before the polish dries.

French polished furniture requires a suitable polish (check instructions on the polish), otherwise the surface becomes smeary.

Some furniture benefits from a polish that feeds the wood and builds up an attractive finish. Rings from the bottom of wet glasses, cups, etc. and liquid spills may require a special polish or 'ring remover'.

The Gleneagles Hotel

Cleaning furniture

Leather/upholstered stools
- vacuum with brush attachment
- use baby cotton buds to clean round buttons
- damp wipe and dry polish leather surface

Upright chairs
- damp wipe and polish dry all wooden parts, including legs
- push out pads of dining chairs and damp wipe any food remains
- vacuum all upholstered areas weekly, but brush off daily

Easy chairs
- as for upright chairs, but lift all cushions daily and brush off
- vacuum under cushions as for rest of chair, weekly
- replace loose cushion, ensuring zip is hidden

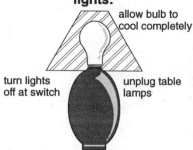
Clean lights

After unplugging or turning off the light (see graphic), use a damp cloth (moistened with a general-purpose cleaner) to lightly wipe:

- the bulb – allow it to cool before touching, otherwise it may no longer work, or even explode

- other parts of the fitting and shade – but paper or fabric shades need extreme care to avoid discolouring or other damage.

For thorough cleaning, shades made of colourfast, washable fabric can be immersed in a cleaning solution, rinsed then left on a draining surface to dry.

 Comfort Inn   Quality Hotel

TV checking/cleaning

1 Switch off television at the plug. Check the plug and wire are in good condition.

2 Wipe top, front, back and sides with a dry cloth and any sticky patches with a damp cloth. Check screen is free from smears and marks.

3 Turn the TV on. Set the sound down to low, and check that each channel is correctly tuned, colour balance and contrast satisfactory. If you have not already done so, check that the remote control is working.

4 Switch the TV off at the mains. Do not leave on stand-by.

Shampoo carpets

Many hotels call in contractors with specialist equipment to shampoo carpets. However this may not be practicable for small hotels, or when just one or two carpets require shampooing.

Follow instructions carefully for the type of machine and the shampoo you are using. Here are some general points:

- vacuum the carpet first, in the normal way, to draw out loose dirt

- shampoo in small sections, overlapping with sections previously cleaned

- avoid over-wetting the carpet

- change shampooing solution as necessary with a large or heavily soiled carpet

- avoid walking over the carpet while damp

- vacuum the carpet after it has dried.

After finishing with the machine, unplug it. Wash out and rinse the tank. Wipe clean the body of the machine and the lead.

For specialist tasks follow carefully the instructions that come with the product (in this example, Johnson Wax floor polish stripper, emulsion floor polish, floor maintainer and floor gloss builder).

Wet shampooing

1 Assemble equipment. Place warning signs. Remove as much furniture as possible. Check carpet is secured at the edges (not necessary with wholly synthetic carpets).

2 Vacuum the carpet to remove loose soil.

3 Check colour fastness, using cleaning agent on a white cloth in one corner.

4 Remove any stains.

5 Place pieces of card, foil or plastic underneath legs of furniture.

6 Open windows and doors to obtain maximum ventilation.

7 Wet and prime shampoo brush.

8 Starting furthest from the door, clean in overlapping passes. Avoid splashing walls and furniture.

9 Clean corners and edges using a scrubbing bush dipped in the cleaning solution.

10 Remove as much water as possible using the wet suction machine.

11 Rinse the carpet systematically. Remove as much water as possible.

12 Pile brush the carpet.

13 Return furniture to original position, place any legs on pieces of card, foil or plastic.

14 When dry, vacuum the carpet.

Stripping floors

1 Add 5 measures stripper to 5 litres cold or warm water.

2 Mop on to floor. Wait 5 minutes.

3 Agitate floor with mop. Wait 5 to 10 minutes.

4 Remove slurry.

5 Allow to dry.

Protecting floors

1 Pour a small amount of polish on to floor or centre of mop.

2 Spread thinly and evenly.

3 Allow to dry thoroughly (about 30 minutes).

4 Apply further coats as needed.

Maintaining floors

1 Dust mop floor.

2 Add 1.5 measures floor maintainer to 5 litres hot or cold water.

3 Damp mop and buff floor.

Alternatively

1 Spray floor with fine mist of floor gloss builder.

2 Buff until dry.

Deal with stains

Ordinary dirt lies on or near the surface, but stains penetrate right into the fibres of carpets, upholstery or material. Catching the stain before it fully soaks in and dries improves the likelihood of removing it.

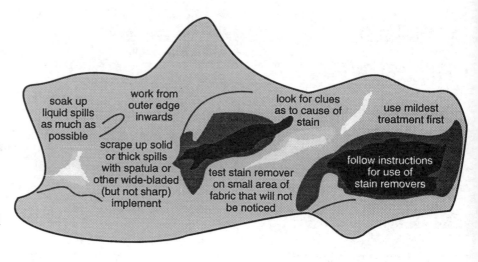

soak up liquid spills as much as possible

work from outer edge inwards

scrape up solid or thick spills with spatula or other wide-bladed (but not sharp) implement

look for clues as to cause of stain

test stain remover on small area of fabric that will not be noticed

use mildest treatment first

follow instructions for use of stain removers

Unfortunately, no stain remover suits every type of stain or fabric. Using the wrong method can spread the stain, and damage and discolour the surrounding fabric.

Remove the stain

If the stain is caused by a liquid spill, which has not yet dried, soak up as much as possible by gently pressing an absorbent cloth (of white material, otherwise the colour may spread) or paper towelling on to the liquid. Work from the outer edges inwards, to avoid spreading the stain.

If the spill is of a thicker consistency, scrape up as much as possible with a spoon, spatula, palette knife, or similar (but not sharp-edged) implement. Avoid digging into or cutting the fabric.

If you do not know the cause of the stain, clues may be provided by its position, colour, consistency and smell.

Mud, for example, is brown, browny-black or browny-red, and tends to cake on the surface of carpets and walls or furniture which people might bump into. A brown liquid spill near the bedside table or drink-making equipment is likely to be tea or coffee. But an empty coke can lying nearby could provide another clue.

If you have established the cause of the stain, test whether the recommended stain remover will harm the fabric, e.g. causing the colour to run (see page 28 for stain-removing tips). With a white cloth, apply some to a small area of the fabric that is unlikely to be noticed. Do not proceed if your cloth picks up the colour of the fabric, or the fabric shows any other ill effect.

If you do not know the cause of the stain, try the mildest treatment first: soaking in cold water. Hot water or detergent may set the stain. If the cold water fails, dry the stain, then apply a solvent.

Treat the stain from the outer edges and work inwards. This reduces the risk of spreading the stain.

Unless the stain remover is one that evaporates, you will need to rinse the affected area with water, then blot dry with an absorbent cloth.

DE VERE
OULTON
HALL
★★★★★
LEEDS

Pressing guest's clothes

1 Within reason, collect the items immediately.

2 Explain to the guest how long it will take. Also explain limitations, e.g. we don't do wedding dresses!

3 All items must either be folded and placed in a clean laundry bag, or placed on a wire hanger. Fasten buttons, zips, etc.

4 Complete a laundry slip for the items pressed. Give the top copy to reception so the charge can be put on the guest's bill. Give the bottom copy to the guest.

Public areas

Where possible, these are cleaned at times few guests and other visitors are about. In some hotels, contractors are used, doing the work late at night or early in the morning.

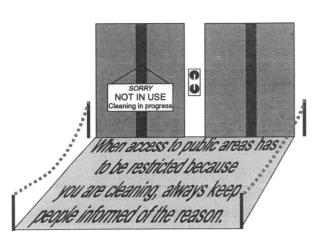

When access to public areas has to be restricted because you are cleaning, always keep people informed of the reason.

Safety first

Place warning signs that cleaning is in progress.

With wide staircases and corridors, or in large foyers, it may be possible to rope off half the area. Guests can continue to use the part you are not cleaning.

Keep the leads of vacuum cleaners, floor polishers, etc. to one side of the corridor, stairs or room.

Always keep cleaning materials or equipment within your sight. If children are about, be especially alert. They can harm themselves by playing with cleaning sprays, for example, or the vacuum machine.

Passenger lifts

Before cleaning a lift:

- switch the control to manual (this needs a special key)

- turn the lift off with the doors open

- place an OUT OF SERVICE FOR CLEANING sign by the lift doors on this and every other floor it serves. If there are two or more lifts, clean one at a time.

Public toilets

Before cleaning public toilets, place a CLEANING IN PROGRESS sign outside the door. With large toilets, which can be cleaned in sections, it is usually sufficient to place signs in the room and cordon off the part you are cleaning.

SWALLOW
ROYAL
HOTEL
BRISTOL

Public toilets: evening routine

1 Collect rubbish, empty waste and sanitary bins.

2 Clean all toilets and urinals.

3 Clean wash hand basins and surrounds, including taps and plug holes. Polish mirrors.

4 Replenish soaps, hand lotions and tissues. Change toilet rolls and ensure there are enough spare. Always check hand towel machines: if red, please change.

5 Clean all floors. Position safety cones while doing this.

Mop sweeping

Equipment

1 mop sweeper
1 vacuum cleaner and attachments
1 dust pan and brush
1 scraper
warning signs

Method for dry floors

1 Assemble equipment.

2 Remove any chewing gum with a scraper.

3 Sweep all areas systematically:

– use a continuous stroke, straight or figure 8, overlapping passes

– keep mop head in contact with floor at all times

– sweep under heavy furniture

– move lighter furniture and replace

– in corners, use dust pan and brush

– when sweeping large areas, collect dirt with pan several times

– if mop sweeper becomes full of dirt, clean it using the vacuum cleaner.

4 Clean equipment (vacuum the mop sweeper head) and return to store.

Care of equipment

• Store mop sweeper head up.

• When dirty, wash mop sweeper head, rinse and hang to dry.

Safety

• Check electrical equipment, particularly plugs and leads.

• Place warning signs in locality.

• Do not leave mop sweeper lying about.

• Check handle is smooth: rough handles may cause splinters.

• When cleaning several rooms, pick up dust after each room. Never move dust from one room to another.

Single solution mopping

Equipment

• any single solution mopping system, i.e. bucket, wringer and mop

• cleaning agent, dispenser and measuring apparatus

1 abrasive pad
1 pair protective gloves
1 scraper
warning signs
bucket cloth

Method

1 Assemble equipment, position warning signs, deal with any chewing gum, and prepare cleaning solution.

2 Apply solution to an area of floor using the mop:

– use a figure 8 stroke, with each pass overlapping

– mop parallel to skirtings

– remove stubborn marks with an abrasive pad

– ensure bucket is behind line of work

– when wringing out mop, stand in front of wringer and press down firmly

– leave floor as dry as possible.

Care of equipment

• Remove mop head from handle, wash and allow to dry. Once reassembled, store head up.

• Wash abrasive pad and allow to dry.

• Wash buckets, wipe and store upside down.

Two solution mopping

• Use second bucket and mop for rinsing water.

• Remove as much cleaning solution from the floor as possible before rinsing.

On mopping floors

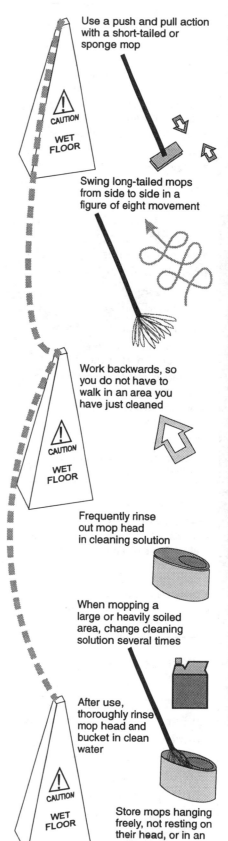

Use a push and pull action with a short-tailed or sponge mop

Swing long-tailed mops from side to side in a figure of eight movement

Work backwards, so you do not have to walk in an area you have just cleaned

Frequently rinse out mop head in cleaning solution

When mopping a large or heavily soiled area, change cleaning solution several times

After use, thoroughly rinse mop head and bucket in clean water

Store mops hanging freely, not resting on their head, or in an empty bucket

Meeting and function rooms

The arrangements will have been agreed in advance with the organisers of the event. By paying careful attention to detail, you can help make sure that everything goes to plan.

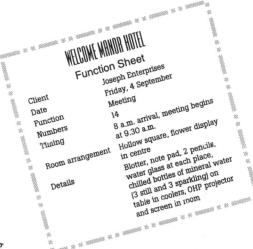

WELCOME MANOR HOTEL
Function Sheet

Client	Joseph Enterprises
Date	Friday, 4 September
Function	Meeting
Numbers	14
Timing	8 a.m. arrival, meeting begins at 9.30 a.m.
Room arrangement	Hollow square, flower display in centre
Details	Blotter, note pad, 2 pencils, water glass at each place, chilled bottles of mineral water (3 still and 3 sparkling) on table in coolers, OHP projector and screen in room

The type of event

The range is wide and there are several variations on each theme. For example, a meeting might involve:

- all those attending sitting around a square table

- another shape table: oblong, round or oval

- a hollow shaped table arrangement, the central floor area filled with flowers

- for larger numbers, and where those at the meeting have different roles, a small 'top' table for the chairperson and/or principal speakers, and many rows of chairs facing this table.

A conference or presentation might be arranged in similar ways, depending on the numbers attending. If there are many people and a need to write notes, there may be tables or a writing surface for each person.

For a special lunch, dinner or working breakfast, the arrangement of tables and chairs might be similar to a small meeting around a table. For larger numbers, there might be a number of individual tables, or an arrangement of large tables.

Possible table and seating arrangements for a small meeting

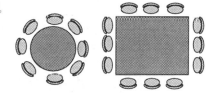

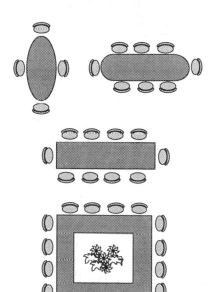

Prepare the room

When events of a similar type often take place in your hotel, you can follow a well established routine. Say it is the regular committee meeting of a local organisation, and 20 people will be attending. You might:

- set up a large table with six chairs on each side and four at each end

- place a flip chart and stand by the top of the table

- cover the table with baize

- put water glasses, bottles of mineral water, pencils or pens, note paper, etc. on the table.

Your hotel may have special furniture for meetings and functions, which can be easily stored and handled (e.g. chairs stacked, tables collapsed). Get help to move heavy and/or difficult to handle items.

When exhibition stands, large floral arrangements, audio visual equipment or other special items are to be set up in the room by other staff or outside contractors, check what access is required. It would waste time if you had put all the chairs and tables out, only to have to move them in order to bring a large stand into the room.

what
What does it mean?

School room or classroom style Seating arranged in parallel rows facing a table at the front of the room. Mostly used for meetings and conferences where those attending are listening to and/or watching speakers standing or sitting at the front of the room. It is possible to get a lot of people into the space available. If delegates need to take notes, tables may be provided, or chairs with a writing surface (e.g. a flip down fixing on the back of the chair, or an extra wide arm rest).

Theatre or cinema style Seating arranged in semicircles (or sometimes straight rows when it is the same as school room style) facing the speaker(s). The seating may be tiered, and/or a raised platform provided for the speakers, as in a theatre or cinema. Tables or writing surfaces may be provided for delegates.

Banquet style Various arrangements of long tables with chairs (see illustration). Mainly used for occasions when those attending are eating, e.g. a luncheon meeting, special dinner or banquet, wedding. By tradition, this is more formal than the dinner dance style. From a practical point of view, it is a way of maximising the number of people that can be seated in the room for a meal.

Dinner dance style Individual tables, usually round, arranged informally around the room. Each table may seat the same number, or there may be variations, so that different sized groups can be at the one table. The dance floor is left clear, but if space is restricted, tables are moved closer together after the meal has finished (during this time, guests retire to another room) and the dance floor is laid in the cleared area.

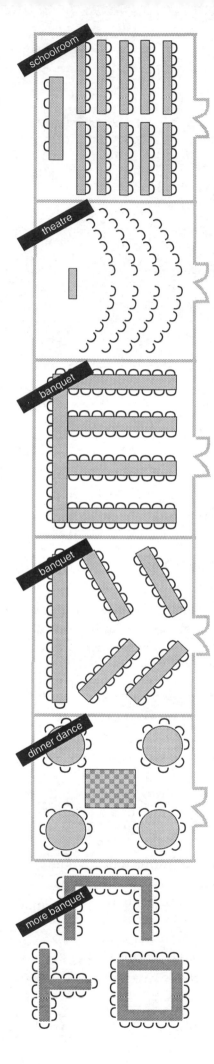

The paperwork

Unless you work in a small hotel, you will have various forms to complete: to report what rooms you have cleaned, to order extra cleaning supplies, to report lost property, and so forth.

Complete forms

If you are using carbon paper to make copies, check that it is in the right place, the correct way up. Use a biro, so the writing comes through clearly on to the copies.

Write neatly. If you make a mistake with a number, write it again and cross out the wrong number. Changing the figure 7 to 1, or a 4 to 8 is likely to confuse.

Cancel forms which you decide to re-write or are not required. So there is no confusion, cross through the form and write CANCELLED across it. Forms without serial numbers (to control their use), may be torn up and thrown away.

Order stock

Do not order more stock than you need. To run out of stock wastes time and disrupts the work of the housekeeping department. But having too much ties up storage space and the business's money. Stock may get damaged because it is stored too long or in cramped conditions.

Be specific about the size and name of product you want. Writing 'cleaning cloths' is no help if there are different colours for specific uses.

Write your name on the form, date and sign (or initial) it. In a large hotel, you may be asked to write what floor or wing you work in.

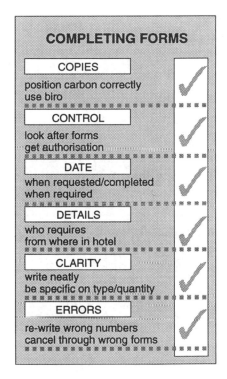

COMPLETING FORMS

COPIES	
position carbon correctly use biro	✓
CONTROL	
look after forms get authorisation	✓
DATE	
when requested/completed when required	✓
DETAILS	
who requires from where in hotel	✓
CLARITY	
write neatly be specific on type/quantity	✓
ERRORS	
re-write wrong numbers cancel through wrong forms	✓

Have the order authorised by your supervisor. Be ready to explain why quantities are much higher or lower than usual.

Take the order to the person or department supplying the items required. There may be set times to do this, or orders received one day are issued the following morning.

Check issues and deliveries of stock

Check against your copy (or the original) of the stock order: have you the number of each type requested?

Once you are satisfied, initial or sign the form to accept the goods. Check that any changes to the quantity of items accepted have been made before you sign.

If you find items which are faulty or damaged, return them before use. When the fault is that of the supplier, a free replacement or refund can be claimed.

Further guidance is given in Section 21.

Complete housekeeping room reports

Update the form as you complete each room. Your supervisor should be able to find out, just by looking at the form, what progress you have made, and which rooms are ready for checking and/or reletting.

As you come across matters which need attention, e.g. a dripping tap, make a note on the form. If you leave this to later, you may forget – especially if a problem or some unexpected change to your plans distracts you.

Use the form to note rooms which have a DO NOT DISTURB notice on the door, and when the guest asks you to come

back at a later time to clean the room. Should the guest complain, e.g. that the room was not cleaned until late in the morning, your correctly completed form will help management deal with the complaint.

Make a note of any unusual events, e.g. signs that two people have slept in a room let as a single, and a stayover room with no personal belongings to indicate that the guest is returning. Even matters which seem insignificant at the time can help in the investigation of problems over the payment of guests' bills or security.

Laundry Weekly Delivery Checklist								
Travel Inn Putney						Week ending 23 April		
Item	1		2					
	Delivery expected	Delivery received	Delivery expected	Delivery received		Weekly total received	Weekly no. of shortages	Weekly no. of rejects
Single sheets	28	28	39	38		230	12	6
Double sheets	34	37	23	23		300	7	1
Pillow cases	89	92	120	122				
Hand towels	98	99	122	127				
Bath towels	90	93	130	128				
Bath mats	89	91	123	122				
Duvet covers			6	6				
Delivery within half an hour of agreed time	Yes	No	Yes	No		Total no. of late deliveries		
	✓			✓		2		

MONTHLY CLEANING	JAN	FEB	MAR	APR
Net curtains washed	3	11	12	18
Ceiling lights cleaned	4	1	14	3
Outside windows cleaned	9	28	21	3
Curtains dusted	11	27	3	

The Angel Inn

HOUSEKEEPING ROOM REPORT

| Name | Jean Vaughan | Date | 12 June |

1 Departure. 1 bed not used. Checked OK. ✓ 8.20 am

2 Stayover. Very untidy. Wet clothes on floor. Muddy boots in bath. ✓ 8.55 am

3 Not occupied. ○

4 Closed for redecoration. ○

5 DO NOT DISTURB notice on door. Still there 12 noon. ○

6 Departure. Cold tap of basin dripping. TV remote control missing. ○ 9.20 am

7 Guest asked not to be disturbed. 9.55 am. ○

8 Departure. OK. ✓ 9.50 am

9 Departure. Stain on bathroom carpet: blood? ○

10 Stayover. OK. ✓ 10.20 am

11 Departure. Lost property report completed (shoes in cupboard). ✓ 11.05 am

12 Departure. Bath towel missing and ashtray. ✓ 11.30 am

Report...

... left or lost property

Describe where and when the item was found and any other details which might help establish who the owner is.

OUT OF ORDER

... faulty equipment, maintenance or repair needs

Give any information which will help identify the problem, e.g. 'vacuum overheating', 'bath plug missing', 'loose hem on right hand bedroom window curtain'.

... injuries

Ask for the accident book or form, so that you can give the details required by law and should you later make a claim to the Department of Social Security for benefits in respect of personal injury or work-related illness (see page 11).

LOST PROPERTY REPORT

Description of item _Teddy bear, honey-coloured, very fluffy_

Where found _Under bed by window in room 303_

When found _12.15 pm 21/8/99_   Who found _Marina Jones_
            TIME   DATE   NAME

Item received for safekeeping by

21 August
DATE   SIGNATURE

MAINTENANCE REPORT

Item _Hair dryer_

Location _Room 45_

Description of fault/problem
Cable damaged (plastic outer covering has melted in two places). Discovered by Terri Jones when checking room.
Report made by _Mrs Waterman_
                        NAME

12 April
DATE   SIGNATURE

ACCIDENT REPORT

Person injured _Max Jasper_

When accident occurred _9.45 am 23/6/9_
                        TIME   DATE

Where accident occurred _In linen room, 1st floor_

Description of accident _Max slipped on floor straining ankle and_

What person injured was doing at time of accident
Max was lifting pile of sheets and bath towels, to load trolley

Names of witness(es)
Mrs Waterman, linen room supervisor

Addresses of witness(es)
_NA_

Report completed by _Mrs Waterman_
                            NAME

Date   Signature
23 June

Receive, store and issue supplies

Stocks of cleaning materials and guest supplies represent considerable value to the business. If the supplier is paid for items never received, profits suffer. Poor control may lead to dishonesty, putting everyone under suspicion.

Prepare for deliveries

The people making the delivery want to get on their way again quickly. The unloading, checking and moving to the storage area need to be done safely. You want to be able to check each item properly, without risk of muddling new stock with old, or stock that is to be returned.

In good time before the delivery is expected:

- clear the delivery area of anything not needed

- put returns aside for collection, counted

- collect trolleys, etc. to help with the moving of stock

- check for safety risks and get these put right (e.g. mop up a spill on the floor)

- have ready your record of what was ordered.

what
What does it mean?

Requisition Form for ordering stock, e.g. of cleaning materials.

Stock rotation A system for ensuring that older stock is used before any more recent stock.

FIFO Stands for FIRST IN FIRST OUT. Used with reference to stock rotation.

Authorisation Obtaining the signature (sometimes an initialled signature is sufficient) of your supervisor or manager or another person with authority to approve your request (e.g. for stocks of cleaning materials).

Stock record form Used to record the quantity of each item, e.g. in the reserve linen stores. It may have columns for STOCK IN or RECEIPTS, e.g. new stock received from the linen supplier, STOCK OUT or ISSUES, e.g. stock issued to the floors to replace damaged linen, the DATE indicating when stock is received or issued, and the BALANCE, i.e. how much stock is left.

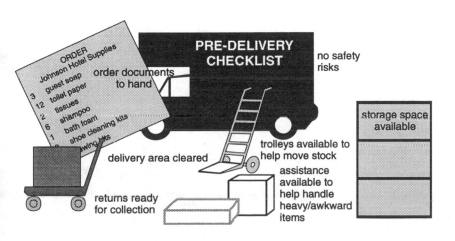

PRE-DELIVERY CHECKLIST

ORDER
Johnson Hotel Supplies
3 guest soap
12 toilet paper
2 tissues
6 shampoo
1 bath foam
shoe cleaning kits
sewing kits

order documents to hand

delivery area cleared

returns ready for collection

no safety risks

storage space available

trolleys available to help move stock

assistance available to help handle heavy/awkward items

Check and sign for deliveries

Do not take short cuts. Even if you know the delivery staff well and find them reliable, it is your responsibility to check the delivery. Most suppliers refuse to consider claims for missing or faulty items if the problem is not identified at the time of delivery.

If it is not provided, ask for the delivery note (sometimes this is the invoice).

1 Check that the items listed agree with your record of what was ordered.

2 Tell your manager at once if the supplier has not delivered the quantity, brand or size requested, so that a decision can be made on what to accept. Special arrangements may have to be made to get the correct stock.

3 When you are satisfied that the delivery can proceed, check as each item is unloaded that the quality is acceptable. Examine the packaging and appearance: do boxes have the stated contents, are bottles full, seals intact, glass or china in perfect condition?

4 Put aside any items which cannot be accepted, or which you are unsure about and need to check with your manager.

5 Count the number of each acceptable item, and tick off against the delivery note.

6 If you get a different total for any item, recount the delivery. If there is still a discrepancy, tell the delivery person. Usually he or she will check.

7 When all is well, sign for the delivery: the delivery person will tell you where to sign if it is not obvious. You will be given a copy of the signed delivery note. Be sure this gets to your manager with no delay.

Deal with problems

When items are unacceptable – wrong size, brand or a quantity or quality problem – the delivery note has to be altered so that the supplier and the people paying the invoice in your company know what has happened. Usually the delivery person will do this, make a note of the reason, and sign against the changes. You then add your signature for the items which have been accepted.

Some suppliers use a returns note for items not accepted on delivery. The delivery person will complete it.

If you disagree with the delivery person over quality or quantity or some other aspect of the delivery, politely ask the person to wait while you call your manager.

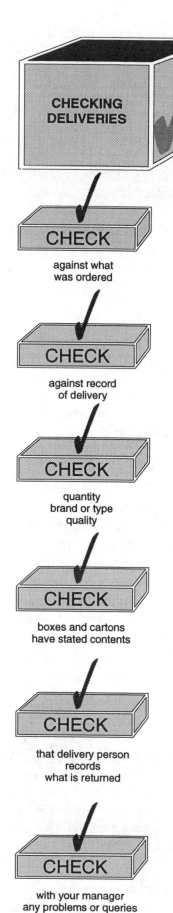

CHECKING DELIVERIES

CHECK
against what was ordered

CHECK
against record of delivery

CHECK
quantity
brand or type
quality

CHECK
boxes and cartons have stated contents

CHECK
that delivery person records what is returned

CHECK
with your manager any problems or queries

Store housekeeping supplies

A wide range of housekeeping supplies are required on a day-to-day basis: cleaning materials and equipment, linen and guest supplies (soap, toilet paper, tissues, etc.). Others are required less frequently: for example blankets, bed boards, cots, winter/summer duvets, replacement lamp shades, curtains, and bed spreads.

Where these items are kept will depend on the space available and how the work of the housekeeping staff is organised. Some hotels have a separate linen room and laundry. There may be smaller stores on each floor, of both cleaning materials and linen. Only authorised staff should have access to the stores. Stores should be locked when left unattended.

Organise storage

- Use the easy-to-reach positions (e.g. shelves at waist height) for items required regularly. Put items which are required infrequently on the highest and lowest shelves.

- Keep similar items together, e.g. furniture polish in one place, glass cleaner in another. With

Housekeeping store
- floors cleaned daily and in good repair
- lights working
- equipment kept clean and in working order
- vacuum cleaners emptied regularly
- sinks left clean and uncluttered
- all cleaning cloths rinsed at the end of the session and hung to dry
- all trolleys and vacuum cleaners returned to the store with the leads folded
- consumables and cleaning materials kept separate and on correct shelving – cleaning materials below consumables
- dirty linen bagged and kept separate, away from clean linen
- black sacks of rubbish into bins at end of a session
- staff coats and handbags stored neatly in specified areas
- notices neatly displayed: COSHH, cleaning procedures and fire safety.

bulky items or those kept in large quantities, it may be necessary to split storage, e.g. unopened cartons on the floor, working stock on the shelf.

- Keep items used for a similar purpose together, e.g. luxury guest supplies for VIP rooms.

- Follow a system for rotating stock, so that the older stock is always used first. This might involve moving the stock already on the shelf to one side, placing the new delivery on the shelf, then putting the older stock back on top.

Store safely

- Follow storage advice on labels, e.g. THIS WAY UP.

- After removing packaging, emptying boxes, take the cardboard, plastic, etc. to the waste collection area.

- Keep walkways free of obstructions.

- Clear up breakages and spills immediately.

- Do not place heavy items or those which are difficult to handle on high shelves.

- Do not leave part-emptied boxes on shelves. This uses more space than necessary, may give a wrong impression about stock levels, and might cause an accident, e.g. if you lift an almost empty box expecting it to be the weight of a full one.

- Where it is necessary to stack cases and boxes on the floor, do not go above shoulder height.

- Use trolleys, steps and other equipment provided. Never stand on boxes or shelves.

- Label equipment awaiting repair or service, and items to be returned to the supplier. Do not store faulty equipment where someone might attempt to use it, unaware of the risk.

- Never store cleaning materials in unlabelled containers, or in containers sometimes used for food or drink.

Housekeeping stores

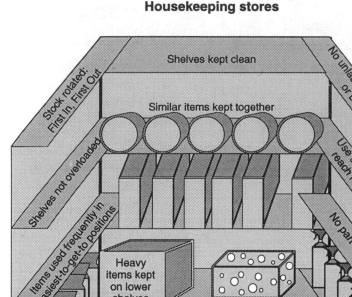

Shelves kept clean

Stock rotated: First In, First Out

Similar items kept together

No unlabelled containers or boxes

Shelves not overloaded

Use steps or ladder to reach high shelves

Items used frequently in easiest-to-get-to positions

No part-empty boxes

Heavy items kept on lower shelves

After unpacking, empty cartons removed

Instructions on Storage advice labels followed

Walkways kept unobstructed

Signs of pests reported

Linen control

The linen used in a hotel is one of the highest cost factors and therefore must be controlled tightly:

- Access to the main linen store must be kept to a minimum with only the housekeeper and linen keeper holding a key. Always ensure the linen room is locked if unattended.
- Keep a minimum stock level on the shelves in accordance with deliveries.
- All deliveries and collections from the laundry must be physically checked in and out. Any differences must be followed through.
- All linen to the housekeeping, restaurant and kitchen must be issued on a 'clean for dirty' basis.
- Linen collection from floors must be carried out regularly, clean and dirty linen kept separate, thus aiding tidiness and safety.
- Linen collected should be sorted, counted and bagged, then checked against the total of linen which left the linen room at the beginning of the day.

Issue housekeeping supplies

Most hotels have a paper-based system to control the issue of cleaning materials, linen and other housekeeping supplies. It provides useful management information, helping to decide, for example, when replacement stocks must be ordered, and in what quantity. It also discourages waste.

Record stock issues

The floor housekeeper (or other appropriate person) completes a requisition with details of what is required and by whom. This might be in a duplicate book, or on a company form.

As required, the requisition is authorised by the executive housekeeper or manager.

The top copy of the requisition goes to the person issuing the stores. One copy is kept by the person requesting the stores.

There may be rules on when requisitions must be received by, and times set aside for collection.

The person taking collection checks that each item is correct against the original requisition, and signs to acknowledge receipt. If the quantity is different, e.g. because stocks are not available, the actual quantity issued/received should be clearly noted.